Days of the Lord

Days of the Lord

II. Spring

Edited by

William G. Storey

HERDER AND HERDER

1966
HERDER AND HERDER NEW YORK
232 Madison Avenue, New York 10016

Original French edition: *Les Jours du Seigneur,* edited by P. Drujon and R. Cappanera, Editions du Témoignage Chrétien, Paris; German edition: *Die Tage des Herrn,* edited by Heinrich Bacht, S.J., Josef Knecht, Frankfurt am Main.

The other volumes of *Days of the Lord* are:
I. Winter
III. Summer and Fall

Grateful acknowledgment is hereby expressed to those publishers who have granted permission to reprint selections from their works. A detailed list of these works appears in the Reference Table at the end of this book.

Library of Congress Catalog Card Number: 65–21941
© 1966 by Herder and Herder, Incorporated
Manufactured in the United States of America

69754

Contents

TEMPORAL

SANCTORAL

Temporal

That day draws near, that saving hour
When all things made anew shall flower;
O let us greet with joyful face
That day which brings us back your grace.
(*Lenten Vesper Hymn*)

SPRING

Nothing is so beautiful as spring—
    When weeds, in wheels, shoot long and lovely and **lush;**
    Thrush's eggs look little low heavens, and thrush
Through the echoing timber does so rinse and wring
The ear, it strikes like lightnings to hear him sing;
The glassy peartree leaves and blooms, they brush
    The descending blue; that blue is all in a rush
With richness; the racing lambs too have fair their fling.

What is all this juice and all this joy?
    A strain of the earth's sweet being in the beginning
In Eden garden.—Have, get, before it cloy,
    Before it cloud, Christ, lord, and sour with sinning,
Innocent mind and Mayday in girl and boy,
    Most, O maid's child, thy choice and worthy the winning.

GERARD MANLEY HOPKINS [1]

Season of Lent

On Ash Wednesday the whole Church closes ranks, so to speak, and prepares in fasting and prayer for the long forty days' journey toward the triumphant Passover. She prepares her children in progressive stages to relive sacramentally the mystery of the passion, death, and resurrection of the Lord. If Christians will in childlike docility set themselves to this school of prayer, if they will open their hearts to the influences of the Holy Spirit, they will come to experience anew the joy and the light of the resurrection and of their baptismal regeneration.

But men find this forty-day trek laborious, as hard as that experienced by the Hebrews during their forty desolate years in the deserts of Sinai when they were so tempted to reject the leadership both of Moses and God and to turn back to the fleshpots of Egypt;[1] as austere as the forty days and nights that Moses spent alone and aloft on the heights of Sinai in preparation for his saving mission;[2] as wearying as the forty-day journey of the prophet Elijah to Horeb, the mountain of God;[3] as purifying and as tiring as the forty days and nights that Jesus Christ spent in the desert.[4]

And yet between the exodus from Egypt and the entry into Chanaan, manna, quail, springing water, and the anticipation of the good things to come appeased their hunger and thirst and relieved their fatigue; Moses was not just hungry and thirsty but surrounded and immersed in the glorious cloud of the Divine

[1] Ex. 16 and 17.
[2] First Lesson, Ember Wednesday of Lent.
[3] Second Lesson, Ember Wednesday of Lent.
[4] Gospel, First Sunday of Lent.

11

Presence; Elijah, although he fell asleep in despair under his juniper tree, hoping that this sleep would be his last, awoke to food brought to him by angels and in the strength of this Godsend walked for forty days and forty nights to Horeb where God appeared to him in that mysterious *whisper of a gentle breeze;*[5] and Jesus himself, finally, was waited upon by angels after His ordeal in the desert.[6]

All Lent lies in the shadows cast by those great scriptural images—images of austerity and trial ending in mercy and salvation.[7] With these examples in mind the Church asks of her children an austere but cheerful fast,[8] a salutary purification of their faults,[9] a concrete manifestation of their contrition,[10] the kind of a fast such as that so magnificently described by the prophet Isaiah.[11]

The Church also foresees that the Lenten battle is not waged just against the weariness of flesh and blood but also against the spiritual powers inimical to man and to his salvation.[12] She knows from certain experience that the fatigue and discouragement which sometimes overwhelm the faithful often stem from their intimate conviction of their innate and apparently incurable sinfulness. Consequently, in the midst of this period of fast and abstinence and spiritual labors, she reminds us again and again of the terminus of the journey, of the transforming conversion which is destined to take place in the light of Easter.[13] To pick up our courage we are reminded of the luminous hope of the resur-

[5] 1 K. 19, 12.

[6] Mt. 4, 11.

[7] Epistle, First Sunday of Lent.

[8] Gospel, Ash Wednesday.

[9] Collects of Thursday of First Week of Lent; of Saturday, Second Week of Lent; of Monday, Third Week of Lent; of Friday, Third Week of Lent; of Wednesday, Fourth Week of Lent.

[10] Epistle, Ash Wednesday.

[11] Epistle of Friday and Saturday after Ash Wednesday.

[12] Collects of Ash Wednesday, of Thursday of Second Week of Lent; Gospel of Saturday after Ash Wednesday and Gospel of Third Sunday of Lent; Communion of Ember Friday; Postcommunion of Ember Wednesday.

[13] See the accounts of resurrection in the Lessons of Thursday and Friday of the Fourth Week of Lent. See the Gospel, Second Sunday of Lent, Offertory of Ember Friday, etc.

rection[14] and of final triumph. The Church is constantly recalling the riches we already possess by way of anticipation:[15] Christ's efficacious Word,[16] His Body and Blood,[17] His Presence in the Christian community,[18] all things so close and familiar to us that we run the constant peril of underestimating their freshness and originality.

But there is more to Lent than a renovation of the Christian spirit and baptismal commitment of the faithful. From the earliest times, Easter was set aside in a unique way for the sacraments of Christian initiation, and Lent grew gradually and progressively into a sacred forty days (quarantine) of catechetical instruction and initiation into the final stages of the catechumenate. It was during this crucial period that the catechumens prepared themselves by a final effort for a new life in Christ. It was then that they underwent the last assaults, the final troubles, the ultimate hesitations in the face of the total commitment which would be demanded of them a few days hence.[19] They still needed to penetrate more deeply into the demands of this Christian religion they were about to embrace, into the heart of that Master to whom they were to surrender themselves irrevocably. They needed to know more of faith in action,[20] of love of one's enemies,[21] and of personal responsibility.[22] The Church hides nothing from them of the deposit of faith which she has received. She speaks to them of the necessity of observing the spirit as well as the letter of the commandments[23] and of the struggles that await them; she reminds them of the gravity of the role they are undertaking: it is a matter of life or death eternal;[24] she recalls how the Chosen People in their blindness could not or would not recognize Jesus

[14] Gospel, Monday of the Second Week of Lent.
[15] Lessons, Ember Saturday.
[16] First Lesson, Tuesday of First Week of Lent.
[17] Gospel, Sunday of the Fourth Week of Lent.
[18] Gospel, Tuesday of the Third Week of Lent.
[19] Gospel, Tuesday of the Second Week of Lent.
[20] Gospel, Monday of the First Week of Lent.
[21] Gospel, Friday after Ash Wednesday.
[22] Epistle, Thursday and Friday after Ash Wednesday.
[23] Epistle and Gospel, Wednesday of the Third Week of Lent.
[24] Epistle and Gospel, Thursday of the Second Week of Lent.

as their Savior while the Ninevites repented at the voice of Jonah, God's prophet, and the Queen of Sheba recognized Solomon, God's wiseman.[25] Will the catechumens recognize Christ? Will they go to him with open eyes and hearts?

Above all, the Church invites them to contemplate the mysterious design of God: the Jews, the Chosen People, were rejected; the Gentiles flooded into the Christian community and became the new people of God.[26] Should these considerations not suggest both that they admire the mysterious activity of the Holy Spirit at work in them, transforming them from pagans into Christians, from children of darkness into children of light,[27] and that they thank Him for this marvellous and purely gratuitous choice?

Laetare (Rejoice!) Sunday opens the fourth week of Lent when the Church can no longer contain her joy: now mere catechumens, they will soon be sons of Mother Church;[28] the community, like Moses of old, intercedes for them before God;[29] purified by repentance, the baptismal waters will grant them a new heart;[30] they will see rebirth as the People of God [31] and Christ's light will dispel their darkness once and for all. God awaits their return from exile more tenderly and faithfully than a mother her children.[32]

[25] Gospel, Wednesday of the First Week of Lent.

[26] The Roman centurion and the Canaanite woman foreshadow the call of the Gentiles (Thursday after Ash Wednesday and Thursday of First Week); the murderous vine-dressers (Friday of Second Week); Jacob as a replacement for his elder brother and the prodigal son (Saturday of Second Week); Naaman the Syrian and the widow of Sarephta, Gentiles for whom miracles were accomplished (Monday of Third Week).

[27] Epistle, Third Sunday of Lent.

[28] Introit, Fourth Sunday of Lent.

[29] Epistle, Tuesday of the Fourth Week of Lent.

[30] Lessons and Gospel, Wednesday of Fourth Week of Lent. This Mass is a pre-baptismal liturgy par excellence, the day of the "Great Scrutiny" when the catechumens took one of their final steps toward their Easter initiation.

[31] The resurrection miracles of the Epistle and Gospels of Thursday and Friday of the Fourth Week of Lent.

[32] Epistle and Gospel, Saturday of the Fourth Week of Lent.

14

For four long weeks the Church presents the Chrstian mystery of death and life. She conducts her children from the temptations in the desert, where Christ chose the cross,[33] to the Transfiguration, an anticipation of the glory to come;[34] from the assaults of Satan[35] to the joy of that community which is constituted by its common feeding upon the eucharistic Body and Blood of Christ.[36] Now she sets before both faithful and catechumens the drama of the blessed passion simply asking them to relive this historic struggle of their Lord which is expressed anew each year liturgically.

The last two weeks of Lent are consecrated to the contemplation of the bruised and persecuted Christ, appealing to the judgment of His Father, to Him who reads the innermost secrets of mind and heart.[37] The liturgy of Passiontide constantly proposes Jeremiah as its prophetic figure.[38] The great legal process involving God and the world unfolds itself before us as we see Christ on trial before the leaders of His people in the readings chosen from John's Gospel.[39] Before our eyes unfolds the great struggle between darkness and light, lies and truth, death and life, Satan and Christ. But the Church, like a good mother, does not abandon us to such anguished considerations. She constantly sets before our eyes the sources of Christian hope: the power of repentance and mortification before God,[40] the even greater power of love,[41] God's great design to gather into one people all His scattered children.[42] And our hope grows as we take part in the procession of palms, a messianic triumph of Christ the Lord. Cross and resurrection are inextricably intertwined all during

[33] Gospel of the Temptation, First Sunday of Lent.

[34] Gospel of the Transfiguration, Second Sunday of Lent.

[35] Gospel, Third Sunday of Lent.

[36] Epistle and Gospel, Fourth Sunday of Lent.

[37] Introits, First Passion Sunday and Monday of Passion Week; Epistle of Holy Thursday.

[38] Epistles, Friday and Saturday of Passion Week, Two of Holy Week.

[39] First Passion Sunday, Monday, and Tuesday of Passion Week.

[40] Epistle, Monday of Passion Week.

[41] The sinful woman: Gospel, Thursday of Passion Week.

[42] Gospel, Friday of Passion Week.

Holy Week.[43] The pathetic elements are certainly present, especially as we hear proclaimed the great passion recitals from the four Gospels; spelled out before us with great simplicity but singular dramatic intensity is the completion of the prophecies of Isaiah about the suffering servant of Yahweh.[44] And yet what issues from the drama of the cross is already known to us and lived by us—believers. But the drama of death and resurrection continues to take place in the hearts of millions of believers each year as they gather in their liturgical assemblies to contemplate Christ crucified, dead, buried, and risen. How many men will consent this year to die with Christ that they may come to life together with Him? How many will renounce all that they might gain all? How many will with conviction say with the Church: Death is the source of life? [45]

ASH WEDNESDAY

Remember, man, that you are dust, and into dust you shall return.
(Distribution of Ashes)

The ashes are a symbol of this passing world, of death. They are a symbol, too, of penance· The practice of sprinkling ashes on the head in token of penance is one which was customary even in the Old Testament. We have the famous example of the inhabitants of Nineveh who took to heart the preaching of the prophet Jonah, and by doing penance in sackcloth and ashes won God's forgiveness and averted His impending wrath. But today the Church has something deeper yet to teach us about the significance of ashes. She takes us back to the first Ash Wednesday in man's history, when God passed sentence upon our fallen humanity: *Cursed is the earth of your work; with labor and toil you shall eat thereof all the days of your life. Thorns and thistles shall it bring forth to you . . . In the sweat of your face shall you eat bread till you return to the ground, out of which you were*

43 Collects of Palm Sunday and of Wednesday of Holy Week; Epistle of Palm Sunday; Introit, Tuesday of Holy Week.

44 Epistle, Wednesday of Holy Week.

45 Postcommunion, Wednesday of Holy Week.

taken: for you are dust, and into dust you shall return. [Gen. 3, 17–19] The Church repeats these words today as she traces the ashen cross upon our foreheads. Thus she strikes the opening chord of a symphony that will resound through all the weeks of Lent, until, in the Easter vigil, it swells to its thrilling climax: "Happy that fault that won so great and glorious a Redeemer." . . .

Humbly, then, yet full of confidence, we go to the altar today to receive the ashen cross upon our foreheads. We are humble because we realize our sinful condition, we who must daily fight against the flesh, surrounded all our lives by sorrow, sin, temptation, and evil. But we are full of confidence, because all the consequences of original sin are transformed by grace, and in the sign of the cross and the triumphant power of grace we shall achieve the final victory.

PIUS PARSCH [2]

Where your treasure is, there your heart also will be. (Gospel)

O man, if you are going to remain here on earth, store up your treasures here. But, if you are going up to heaven, why do you leave them here below? The man caring for treasures destined to be left behind is caring for others' treasures, not his own. Living here below, where we are pilgrims, we find it rather hard to be poor, sad, and without honor, even for a while. Then, when we shall be among the eternal citizens of our everlasting country, what will it be like for us to endure pain because of our showing contempt, punishment because of ignobility, shame over our nakedness? What will it be like to be sentenced to torments when others are being promoted into possession of the kingdom? When the poor man is led to sit with God, and the rich man is dragged to the assembly of the damned? Oh, how lamentable will be the reversal of the situation when those whom men despaired of will acquire hope divine, and those who possessed human treasures will defraud themselves of the heavenly ones!

All this is what that treasure brings about. Either through alms-giving it raises the heart of a man into heaven, or through avarice it buries it in the earth. That is why He said: *For where*

17

your treasure is, there your heart also will be. [Mt. 6, 21] O man, send your treasure on, send it ahead into heaven, lest you bury your God-given soul in the earth. Gold comes from the depth of the earth; the soul, from the highest heaven. Clearly, it is better to carry the gold to the abode of the soul than to bury the soul in the mine of the gold. That is why God orders those who will serve in His army here below to fight as men stripped of concern for riches and unencumbered by anything. To these He has granted the privilege of reigning in heaven.

ST. PETER CHRYSOLOGUS [3]

Prayer and mortification are the two wings by which, with the grace of God, the soul rises and reaches the summit of perfection.

ST. ALPHONSUS RODRIGUEZ [4]

THURSDAY AFTER ASH WEDNESDAY

O Lord, hear my prayer. (Introit)

Like travellers lost in a parched and burning desert,
　　We cry unto you, O Lord.

Like men shipwrecked on a lonely coast,
　　We cry unto you, O Lord.

Like a father robbed of a crust of bread that he was
　　bringing to his starving children,
　　　　We cry unto you, O Lord.

Like a prisoner unjustly confined to a dank and
　　gloomy dungeon,
　　　　We cry unto you, O Lord.

Like a slave torn by his master's lash,
　　We cry unto you, O Lord.

18

Like an innocent man led to execution,
 We cry unto you, O Lord.

Like all the nations of the earth before the day of
 their deliverance dawned,
  We cry unto you, O Lord.

Like Christ on the Cross when he said: "My God,
 My God, why have you forsaken me?"
  We cry unto you, O Lord.

FELICITE DE LAMENNAIS [5]

The necessity for prayer.

The Trinity is nigh unto all things, and yet not all things are nigh
unto It. Only with holy prayers and pure minds and with souls
prepared for union with the Godhead do we come nigh to It; for It
is not in space, so as to be absent from any spot, or to move from
from one position to another, and to speak of It as omnipresent
does not express this all-transcendent and all-embracing infini-
tude. But let us press on in prayer, always thirsting for the divine
benignant rays·

As if a luminous chain hung suspended from the heights of
heaven and reached down to this world below, and we by seiz-
ing it, first with one hand, then with the other, seemed to be
pulling it down, but in very truth instead of pulling it down, we
found ourselves carried upward to the higher splendors of the
shining rays.

Or as if we were on a ship, clinging to the ropes which bound
the ship to some rocks, and we were pulling on the ropes, but we
would not be drawing the rocks toward our ship, but in very
truth we would be pulling the vessel close to the rocks.

Or as if we were standing on a ship pushing away the rock on
shore, but we would not be affecting the immovable rock, for in
very truth we would be separating ourselves from it; and the
more we push it, the more we would be warding it off.

So it is, before every endeavor and especially those endeavors
which concern divinity, we must begin with prayer: not to pull

down to ourselves what is nigh both everywhere and nowhere, but to commend and unite ourselves to God by these invocations and remembrances.

DENIS THE AREOPAGITE [6]

FRIDAY AFTER ASH WEDNESDAY

Be perfect as your heavenly Father is perfect. (Gospel)

Before the eyes of God two groups, and two only, constitute the world of souls: those who on the one hand have life that is supernatural, those who on the other hand are alien to that life. And from God's point of view there is an immensely greater distance between the best of pagans and the most humble of Christians than between the very least among the faithful and our Holy Father the Pope.

Why then should perfection be looked upon as being something like a world apart, a closed corporation from which lay folk should very naturally be excluded. "This distinction," writes St. John Chrysostom, "exists nowhere in the Gospel. Our Lord there names neither religious nor seculars; this distinction has been introduced by the imagination of men. The Scriptures have no mention to make of anything like that; they intend that all men *aspire* to lead the same life, be they solitaries or married. *For we are all obliged to aspire to the same perfection.* It is a necessity then for the man living in the world, as for the monk, to live according to the manner of a Christian and to tend to a perfection which is the same for both."

In thus rendering the laymen the supernatural dignity due him, we are heightening his ideals. Nobility of nature carries its own obligation—*noblesse oblige*. Raised as he is to an order of living infinitely superior to the natural, endowed with a life that is supernatural, participating in the intimate life of God Himself—it all signifies that the Christian is expected to live after a manner quite different indeed from the manner of the pagan unequipped with such prerogatives. His conduct, his customs, his

20

manners should be those of a child of God, of a member of Jesus Christ, of a temple of the Holy Ghost.

Made to understand his proper rank and place, which is that of child of God, the lay person whoever he be, sees he is obliged to be perfect, that is, to tend to perfection, quite as much as any priest or religious. St. John Chrysostom has just reminded us of that: we are obliged to tend to perfection because of our dignity of Christian. Just as a child will naturally imitate his father so the baptized lay person must strive to live like God, to comport himself like God. As each member of the human body must follow the directions of the head of that body and act in conformity with it, so the Christian, the disciple of Christ, the member of the Mystical Body of which Jesus is the Head, must endeavor to make his activity conformable to the activity of the Whole—he should comport himself according to the directions that come to him from the Head and show himself in everything worthy of the holiness of the Body of which he is part.

Let us have done with entertaining the idea that Christian perfection, or holiness, is quite all right for priests and religious, but that this obligation of tending to perfection is not applicable to ordinary lay folk. The fact is that every person who has received supernatural life through God's unspeakable privilege in Baptism, is held bound to cultivate that life, to develop it and cause it to grow to its plenitude, which is nothing other than holiness. Just as the plant develops unceasingly with a view to producing its flower and fruit, so must the soul supernaturalized by the grace of Baptism tend to blossom into the flower and fruit of holiness. Or to use another figure: just as the brook winds its way to the river and finally to the ocean, so must the supernaturalized soul press forward with all its strength to its proper fulness of growth, which is perfection.

NORBERT ROBICHAUD [7]

All are called to perfection.

Lay sanctity is to be forged from cars that won't start in the morning, from babies that cry to be fed and changed, from children that need the reassurance that comes from being listened to with love or lifted with loving arms, from the long trek back and forth to work, from the community meeting at which more meetings are planned. Sanctity for the layman can only be achieved from the broken pieces of an untidy day.

DENNIS GEANEY [8]

SATURDAY AFER ASH WEDNESDAY

The Gospel of the day then sets before us the duty of *faith,* and rests it upon God's almightiness or omnipotence, as it is called. Nothing is too hard for Him, and we believe what the Church tells us of His deeds and providences, because He can do whatsoever He will. But there is another grace which the Gospel teaches us, and that is *hope* or *trust.* You observe that when the storm came, the disciples were in great *distress.* They thought some great calamity was coming on them. Therefore Christ said to them, *Why are you fearful?* [Mk. 4, 40] Hope and fear are contrary to each other; they feared because they did not hope. To hope is not only to believe in God, but to believe and be certain that He loves us and means well to us, and therefore it is a great Christian grace. For faith without hope is not certain to bring us to Christ. *The devils also believe and tremble* [Jas. 2, 19]. They believe, but they do not come to Christ—because they do not hope, but despair. They despair of getting any good from Him. Rather they know that they shall get nothing but evil, so they keep away. You recollect the man possessed of the devil said: *What have we to do with You, Jesus the Son of God —are You coming to torment us before the time?* [Mt. 8, 29]. The coming of Christ was no comfort to them, the contrary: they shrank from Him. They knew He meant them not good, but punishment. But to men He meant good, and it is by knowing and feeling this that men are brought to Him. They will not come to God till they are sure of this. They must believe that He is not only almighty, but all merciful also. Faith is founded on the knowledge that God is almighty, hope is founded on the knowledge that God is all merciful. And the presence of our Lord and Saviour Jesus Christ excites us to hope quite as much as to faith, because His very name Jesus means Saviour, and be-

22

cause He was so loving, meek, and bountiful when He was on earth.

He said to the disciples when the storm arose, *Why are you fearful?* That is, you ought to hope, you ought to trust, you ought to repose your heart on Me. I am not only almighty, but I am all merciful. I have come on earth because I am most loving to you. Why am I here, why am I in human flesh, why have I these hands which I stretch out to you, why have I these eyes from which the tears of pity flow, except that I wish you well, that I wish to save you? The storm cannot hurt you if I am with you. Can you be better placed than under my protection? Do you doubt My power or My will, do think Me *negligent* of you that I sleep in the ship, and *unable* to help you except I am awake? Wherefore do you doubt? Wherefore do you fear? Have I been so long with you, and you do not yet trust Me, and cannot remain in peace and quiet by My side?

JOHN HENRY NEWMAN [9]

It is I, do not be afraid. (Gospel)

Man, alas, is above all frightened of God. He is afraid of being burned at his touch, like the Israelites who touched the Ark. That adds subtlety to his denials, cunning to his attempted escapes, and makes the pious inventive in devotional tricks to deaden the shock. . . . Whether incredulous, indifferent or believers, we compete with one another in ingeniously guarding ourselves against God.

HENRI DE LUBAC [10]

FIRST SUNDAY IN LENT

Jesus fasted for forty days and forty nights. (Gospel)

Fasting is only one branch of a large and momentous duty, the subdual of ourselves to Christ. We must surrender to Him all we have, all we are. We must keep nothing back. We must present to Him as captive prisoners with whom He may do what He will, our soul and body, our reason, our judgment, our affections, our imagination, our tastes, our appetite. The great thing is to *subdue* ourselves; but as to the particular form in which the great precept of self-conquest and self-surrender is to be expressed, that depends on the person himself, and on the time or place. What is good for one age or person, is not good for another. . . .

A civilized age is more exposed to subtle sins than a rude age. Why? For this simple reason, because it is more fertile in excuses and evasions. It can defend error, and hence can blind the eyes of those who have not very careful consciences. It can make error plausible, it can make vice look like virtue. It dignifies sin by fine names; it calls avarice proper care of one's family, or industry, it calls pride independence, it calls ambition greatness of mind; resentment it calls proper spirit and sense of honour, and so on.

Such is this age, and hence our self-denial must be very different from what was necessary for a rude age. Barbarians lately converted, or warlike multitudes, of fierce spirit and robust power—nothing can tame them better than fasting. But we are very different. Whether from the natural course of centuries or from our mode of living, from the largeness of our towns or other causes, so it is that our powers are weak and we cannot bear what our ancestors did. Then again what numbers there are who anyhow must have dispensation, whether because their labour is so hard, or because they never have enough, and cannot be called on to stint themselves in Lent. These are reasons for the rule of fasting not being so strict as once it was. And let me now say, that the rule which the Church now gives us, though indulgent, yet is strict too. It tries a man. One meal a day is trial to most people, even though on some days meat is allowed. It is sufficient, with our weak frames, to be a mortification of sensuality. It serves that end for which all fasting was instituted. On the other hand its being so light as it is, so much lighter than it was in former times, is a suggestion to us that there are other sins and weaknesses to mortify in us besides gluttony and drunkenness. It is a suggestion to us, while we strive to be pure and un-

24

defiled in our bodies, to be on our guard lest we are unclean and sinful in our intellects, in our affections, in our wills.

JOHN HENRY NEWMAN [11]

The entire Mystical Body is inspired today by the example of its divine Head, who fasted forty days and forty nights in the desert into which the Spirit of God had led Him; and who triumphed over the tempter, the devil of sensuality, the devil of pride, the devil of rebellion. Christ came not to be *bread*-Messias, a *pomp*-Messias, a *wealth*-Messias. He came to do the will of Him that sent Him. He came to save the world. He came to empty Himself so that empty hearts might have the fulness of life.

But Christ's fast and His victory over satan are not only an *example* for us, they are the source of *sanctification* of our every honest and worthy lenten effort. By His fast He sanctified ours, by His victorious struggle He enables us to be successful in ours. In fact, *our* fast and fight are valuable and holy because they are a participation in the all-holy fast and fight of our divine Head.

We are God's children. He has given His angels charge over us, to keep us in all our ways. The Lord Himself will overshadow us with His shoulders and take us under His eucharistic wing during this acceptable time. In that we trust. On that we depend.

"This holy fast [Quadragesima] will open unto us the gates of Paradise. Let us, therefore, embrace it with prayer and supplication, so that we may rejoice with the Lord on the day of resurrection" (Breviary).

MARTIN B. HELLRIEGEL [12]

MONDAY OF THE FIRST WEEK IN LENT

The profound conversion of individuals and even the practice of virtue depend so much on the transformation of their living conditions that it would be futile to endeavor to lead souls to heaven as if eatrh did not exist. Our Lord was the first to have compassion on the crowd:

He began by giving bread.

Dr. Aujoulat

Lord, give to us,
give to all men their daily bread.
To all men,
not only our loved ones, our neighbors, our countrymen.
To all men,
those countless thousands scattered throughout the world
who never have enough to eat
who are hungry all day, every day.
Give us this day our daily bread.

To this father of nine in the Casbah,
too poor to buy enough bread for the whole family.
(How explain to tearful, hungry children
the anguish of a father's helpless refusal?)
Give us this day our daily bread.
To that impoverished family in a far-off village of Togo
whose only meal a day
the year long
is a bowl of millet.
Give us this day our daily bread.

To all those in every part of Africa, Asia, Europe, America
who do not know what it is like not to be hungry.
Give us this day our daily bread.
Lord, how speak to them of conversion?
How expect of them the practice of virtue?
When You were on earth
did You not begin by giving bread
to those who were hungry?
And Jesus took the loaves:
and when He had given thanks, He distributed
to them that were set down.
And to us
who know that there will be a meal waiting for us this evening,
grant the grace
to think of those millions who are starving.

Grant us the desire
to share with them our daily bread.
To us
who do not know what it means to suffer from hunger
grant the grace
to hear from Your lips at the Last Judgment:
Come, you blessed of My Father,
I was hungry and you gave Me to eat.

SISTER JACQUES DE COMPOSTELLE [13]

What you have done for one of the least of my brethren you have done for me. (Gospel)

Behold an admirable mystery. Jesus needs nothing and Jesus needs all. Because of his power Jesus needs nothing, but because of his compassion he needs everything. *Behold I tell you a great mystery* [Eph. 5, 32], the central mystery of the New Testament. The same mercy which obliged Jesus, innocent as he was, to take upon himself all the crimes of the human race, also obliged him, happy as he is, to take upon himself all our miseries. Just as the most innocent has borne the most sin, so too the most bountiful suffers the most need. He is hungry and he is thirsty; he groans in chains; he labors under maladies; he suffers both heat and cold at one and the same time. Truly poor he is the poorest of the poor, because all other poor persons simply suffer themselves while there is only Jesus Christ who experiences all that men suffer.

JACQUES BOSSUET [14]

It will not be by countering doctrine with doctrine, by matching ritual against ritual that the reconciliation of all Christians will be initially fostered. It will only be by the Christ-image in our own lives. We cannot afford to count the personal cost in living the life of Christ again on Main Street. "Here one has to drink one's Christianity straight." "This is very good and wholesome but one still lifts the terrible glass with a trembling hand and a tearful eye to the lips—the terrible glass filled to the brim with the terrible Christian verities." Fundamentally essential

27

as doctrine most certainly is, how many new Catholics embrace the old Faith because of the intellectual attraction of one of its dogmas?

The burning issue in the minds of despairing millions today is not the acceptability of Catholic dogma. It is simply this: can genuine Christianity solve the social, economic, and moral conflicts of our times? Does the embittered zealot of the picket line for example, give a snap of his fingers for the pro's and con's of Purgatory and indulgences? Does the harrowed millionaire contemplating the pavement below from the parapet of his penthouse worry about the Virgin Birth and the Immaculate Conception? Does the bewildered bootblack, sliding his fingers across the grease of a shoeshine can, fret about the canon of Holy Scripture?

People today are not drawn to Christ by theological filibustering which clouds the main issue—can genuine Christianity work? Jesus Christ did not speak in syllogisms. He went down among the poor, the sick, and the wayward with gentle compassion and understanding, drawing them to Himself with the sweetness of His charity. Page back through Christian history to those primitive days when Christianity was, in the truest sense of the word, reforming, "giving new form" to the pagan world. Those thousands of converts were not attracted to Christianity by semantics and oratory; they heard of the love of Christ and saw how Christians loved one another. They saw Christians sharing their surplus property with the poor, sanctifying the home by the substitution of the Holy Family for the old lares and penates of the hearth, joyfully singing in the depths of their dungeons and rushing eagerly onto the hallowed sands of the arena. Not doctrine, not definition, not dogma, cried Tertullian, but "the blood of martyrs is the seed of the Church."

JAMES A. GRIFFIN [15]

TUESDAY OF THE FIRST WEEK IN LENT

Let the wicked man forsake his way . . . and let him return to the Lord, . . . for he is generous in forgiving. (I Lesson)

God, the Master and Maker of the universe, who made all things and determined the proper place of each, showed himself to be long-suffering, as well as a true friend of man. But in fact he always was and is and will be just this—kind and good and slow to anger and true; indeed, he alone is good. And when he had planned a great and unutterable design, he communicated it to his Child alone. Now, as long as he kept back his own wise counsel as a well-guarded mystery, he seemed to be neglecting us and to take no interest in us; but when he revealed it through his beloved Child and made known the things that had been prepared from the beginning, he granted us all things at once. He made us both to share in his blessings and to see and understand things that none of us could ever have looked for.

And so, when he had planned everything by himself in union with his Child, he still allowed us, through the former time, to be carried away by undisciplined impulses, captivated by pleasures and lusts, just as we pleased. That does not mean that he took any delight in our sins, but only that he showed patience. He did not approve at all of that season of wickedness, but on the contrary, all the time he was creating the present age of righteousness, so that we, who in the past had by our own actions been proved unworthy of life, might now be deemed worthy, thanks to God's goodness. Then, when we had shown ourselves incapable of entering the Kingdom of God by our own efforts, we might be made capable of doing so by the power of God. And so, when our unrighteousness had come to its full term, and it had become perfectly plain that its recompense of punishment and death had to be expected, then the season arrived in which God had determined to show at last his goodness and power. O the overflowing kindness and love of God toward man! God did not hate us, or drive us away, or bear us ill will. Rather, he was long-suffering and forbearing. In his mercy, he took up the burden of our sins. He himself gave up his own Son as a ransom for us—the holy one for the unjust, the innocent for the guilty, the righteous one for the unrighteous, the incorruptible for the corruptible, the immortal for the mortal. For what else could cover our sins except his righteousness? In whom could we, lawless and impious as we were, be made righteous except in the Son of God alone? O sweetest exchange! O unfathomable work of God! O blessings beyond all expectation! The sinfulness of many is hidden in the Righteous One, while the righteousness of the One justifies the many that are sinners. In the former time he had proved to us our nature's inability to gain life; now he showed the Saviour's power to save even the powerless, with the intention that on both counts we should have faith in his goodness, and look on him as Nurse, Father, Teacher, Counselor, Healer, Mind, Light, Honor, Glory, Might, Life—and that we should not be anxious about clothing and food.

LETTER TO DIOGNETUS [16]

You have made my house a den of thieves. (Gospel)

To reject God because man has corrupted the idea of God, and religion because of the abuse made of it, is the effect of a sort of clear-sightedness which is yet blind. For surely the holiest things are inevitably destined to be the victims of the worst abuses. Religion, which is its own source and origin, must continue to purify itself. Moreover, under one form or another man always turns back to adoration. It is not merely his first duty but his deepest need. It is something he cannot extirpate; he can only corrupt it. God is the pole that draws him, and even those who deny him in spite of feeling that attraction, bear witness to him.

HENRI DE LUBAC [17]

In the state of self-abandonment the one rule is the present moment. The soul is as light as a feather, as fluid as water, simple as a child, as easily moved as a ball, so as to receive and follow all the impressions of grace. Abandoned souls have no more hardness or consistency than melted metal. For just as metal takes all the shapes of the mould into which it is poured, these souls adapt and adjust themselves as easily to all the forms which God wishes to give them. In a word, their disposition resembles that of the air which is at the service of all who breathe it and of water which takes the form of every recipient.

They present themselves to God like a perfectly plain and simple canvas, without concerning themselves to know the subject which it may please God to paint in their souls, for they trust themselves to Him, they are abandoned and wholly occupied with their duty, think neither of themselves nor of what is necessary for them, nor of how they are to procure it. The more, however, they apply themselves to their little job, so simple, so hidden, so contemptible (as its outward appearances may be), the more God diversifies and beautifies it. On the background of simple love and obedience, His hands love to trace the most beautiful details, the most delicate and exquisite drawings, the most Divine figures: *Mirificavit Dominus Sanctum suum*. A canvas which is simply blindly abandoned to the painter's brush, merely receives each moment the impact of the brush. Similarly if a stone could feel it would feel nothing but the cruel point of the tool destroying it, but in no case the figure of which it is tracing the lineaments.

Yes, dear souls, simple souls, leave to God what belongs to Him and remain loving and passive under His action. Hold for certain that what happens to you internally and externally is for the best. Leave God to act and abandon yourselves to Him. Let the point of the knife and the needle work. Let the brush of the Master cover you with a variety of colours which seem only to disfigure the canvas of your soul. Correspond with all these Divine operations by the uniform and simple disposition of a complete self-abandonment, self-forgetfulness and application to your duty. Keep to the line of your own advance and, without knowing the map of the country or the details, names and directions of the land you are passing through, walk blindly along that line and everything will be indicated to you if you remain passive. Seek only the Kingdom of God and His justice in love and obedience and all the rest will be given you.

JEAN PIERRE DE CAUSSADE [18]

31

EMBER WEDNESDAY IN LENT

Whoever does the will of my heavenly Father, that person is brother and sister and mother to me. (Gospel)

God has called you to the same things; He has not given more to one than to another. He has granted immortality to all, eternal life to all, undying glory to all, brotherhood to all, and inheritance to all. He has become the common head of all, He has made all to rise together and to sit down together. Therefore, since you have such equality of honor in the things of the spirit, how is it that you are proud? Is it because So-and-so is wealthy and So-and-so is strong? How ridiculous this is! Tell me this. If the emperor were to take ten men, clothe them in purple robes, and seat them on the imperial throne, would any one of them dare to revile another because he was more wealthy or more illustrious? By no means! I have not yet told you everything, for the difference is not so great. If, then, we are equal in heaven, are we different on earth? *One Lord, one faith, one baptism.* There is the hope of your calling. *One God and Father of all, who is above all, and throughout all, and in us all.* [Eph. 4, 5–6] No one is called greater for you but less for that man, is he? you were not saved by faith and he by works, were you? Was your sin forgiven in baptism, while his sin was not? Heaven forbid! *One God and Father of all, who is above all, and throughout all, and in us all. Who is above all,* that is, God is superior to all; *and throughout all,* that is, by His providence and governance; *and in us all,* that is, because He dwells in all of us.
ST. JOHN CHRYSOSTOM [19]

Penance is the foundation and bearer of true peace detaching men from earthly and perishable goods, lifting them up to goods that are eternal, giving them, even in the midst of privations and adversity, a peace that the world with all its wealth and pleasures cannot give. One of the most pleasing and joyous songs ever heard in this vale of tears is without doubt the famous "Canticle of the Sun" of St. Francis. Now the man who composed it, who wrote and sang it, was one of the greatest penitents, the Poor Man of Assisi, who possessed absolutely nothing on earth, and bore in his emaciated body the painful stigmata of his crucified Lord.

Prayer then and penance are the two potent inspirations sent to us at this time by God, that we may lead back to Him mankind that has gone astray and wanders about without a guide; they are the inspirations that will dispel and remedy the first and principle cause of every revolt and every revolution, the revolt of man against God. But the peoples themselves are called upon to make up their minds to a definite choice; either they entrust themselves to these benevolent and beneficent inspirations and are converted, humble and repentant, to the Lord and the Father of Mercies, or they abandon themselves and what little remains of happiness on earth to the mercy of the enemy of God, to the spirit of vengeance and destruction.

PIUS XI [20]

THURSDAY OF THE FIRST WEEK IN LENT

Have pity on me, Lord, Son of David. (Gospel)

O my Lord Jesus Christ, most loving Spouse, most pure Lover and Governor of every creature, who will give me wings of perfect liberty, so that I may fly high and rest in you? Oh, when shall I fully tend to You and see and feel how sweet You are? When shall I recollect myself so perfectly that I shall not, for Your love, recognize myself, but You alone above myself and above all physical things? You will visit me in such manner as You visit Your faithful lovers. Now, I often mourn and complain of the miseries of this life, and with sorrow and woe bear them with truly great melancholy, for many evil things happen daily in this life which trouble me and greatly darken my understanding. They hinder me greatly, and put my mind away from You, and encumber me so in many ways that I cannot have a free mind and clear desire toward You, or have the sweet embrace that is always present to Your blessed saints. Wherefore, I beseech You, Lord, that the sighing and the inward desire of my heart, together with my many desolations, may somewhat move You and incline You to hear me.

O Jesus, the light and brightness of everlasting glory, the joy and comfort of all Christian people who walk and labor like pilgrims in the wickedness of this world, my heart cries to You by silent desires, without voice; my silence speaks to You and says: How long does my Lord God delay to come? Truly, I trust that He will shortly come to me, His poorest servant, and comfort me and make me joyful and glad in Himself, and deliver me from all anguish and sorrow. Come, Lord, come, for without You I have no glad day or hour. You are all my joy and gladness, and without You my soul is barren and empty. I am a wretch and, as it were, in prison and bound with fetters until You, through the light of Your gracious presence, deign to visit me and to refresh me, to bring me again to liberty of spirit and to show me Your favorable and lovely countenance. Let others seek what they will, but truly, there is nothing I shall seek, or that will please me but You, my Lord God, my hope and everlasting help. I shall not cease my prayer until Your grace return to me, and until You speak inwardly to my soul and say: Lo, I am here; I am come to you because you have called Me. Your tears and the desires of your heart, your humility and your contrition, have bowed Me down and brought Me to you.

And I shall say in return: Lord, I have called You and I have desired to have You. I am ready to forsake all things for You, for You first stirred me to seek You. Wherefore, be You always blessed, who have shown such goodness to me according to the multitude of Your mercies. What has Your servant, Lord, to do or say more, save to humble himself before Your majesty and ever to have in mind his own iniquities? There is none like to You, Lord, in heaven or on earth. Your works are good, Your judgments are wise and just, and Your providence governs all things. Wherefore, to You, Who are the wisdom of the Father, be everlasting joy and glory. I humbly beseech You that my body and my soul, my heart and my tongue and all your creatures may always praise You and bless You.

THOMAS A KEMPIS [21]

EMBER FRIDAY IN LENT

See, you are cured. Sin no more. (Gospel)

And after this He suffereth some of us to fall more hard and more grievously than ever we did afore, as us thinketh. And then we think (who be not all wise) that all were naught that we have begun. But it is not so. For it needeth us to fall, and it needeth us to see it. For if we never fell, we should not know how feeble and how wretched we are of our self, and also we should not fully know that marvellous love of our Maker. For we shall see verily in heaven, without end, that we have grievously sinned in this life, and notwithstanding this, we shall see that were never hurt in His love, nor were the less of price in His sight. And by the assay of this falling we shall have an high, marvellous knowing of love in God, without end. For hard and marvellous is that love which may not, nor will not, be broken for trespass. And this is one understanding of profit. Another is the lowness and meekness that we shall get by the sight of our falling: for thereby we shall highly be raised in heaven; to which raising we might never have come without that meekness. And therefore it needeth us to see it; and if we see it not, though we fell it should not profit us. And commonly, first we fall and later we see it: and both of the Mercy of God.

The mother may suffer the child to fall sometimes, and be diseased [distressed] in diverse manners for its own profit, but she may never suffer that any manner of peril come to the child, for love. And though our earthly mother may suffer her child to perish, our heavenly Mother, Jesus, may not suffer us that are His children to perish: for He is All-Mighty, All-wisdom, and All-love; and so is none but He—blessed may He be!

But oftentimes when our falling and our wretchedness is showed us, we are so sore adread, and so greatly ashamed of our self, that scarcely we wit where we may hold us. But then willeth not our courteous Mother that we flee away, for Him were nothing lother [nothing could displease Him more]. But He willeth then that we use the condition of a child: for when it is diseased, or adread, it runneth hastily to the mother for help, with all its might. So willeth He that we do, as a meek child saying thus: "My kind Mother, my Gracious Mother, my dearworthy Mother, have mercy on me: I have made myself foul and unlike to thee, and I nor may nor can amend it but with thy privy help and grace." And if we feel us not then eased forthwith, be we sure that He useth the condition of a wise mother. For if He see that it be more profit to us to mourn and to weep, He suffereth it, with ruth and pity, unto the best time, for love. And He willeth then that we use the property of a child, that evermore kindly trusteth to the love of the mother in weal and in woe.

JULIAN OF NORWICH [22]

TO GOD THE FATHER

Wilt Thou forgive that sin through which I begun,
   Which was my sin, though it were done before?
Wilt Thou forgive that sin through which I run,
   And do run still, though still I do deplore?
When Thou hast done, Thou hast not done,
                For I have more.

Wilt Thou forgive that sin, which I have won
   Others to sin, and made my sin their door?
Wilt Thou forgive that sin which I did shun
   A year or two: —but wallow'd in a score?
When Thou hast done, Thou hast not done,
                For I have more.

I have a sin of fear, that when I've spun
   My last thread, I shall perish on the shore;
But swear by Thyself, that at my death Thy Son
   Shall shine as He shines now, and heretofore;
And having done that, Thou hast done,
              I fear no more.

JOHN DONNE [23]

EMBER SATURDAY IN LENT

Always try to do good to one another. (Epistle)

Personal faith and fidelity to Christ are not enough to make us perfect Christians. We do not go by ourselves to him, as isolated individuals. We go to him as members of his Mystical Body. It can be said that our holiness is proportioned to our capacity to serve as instruments of his love in establishing his kingdom and building up his Mystical Body. The more fruitful and healthy are our lives as members of Christ, the more we are able to communicate the Christ-life to others, in and through the Holy Spirit. The more we are able to give them, the more we receive from Christ. All the secret influx of mystical life into our souls is intended not only for ourselves but for others. Those who receive the most are those who have the most to give, and if they have more to give it is perhaps because more has been forgiven them [Lk. 7, 47–48]. They have a greater capacity to love Christ in their brother because they have a deeper and more intimate experience of their own sorrow and of his mercy. Suffering and spiritual poverty have taught them compassion and made them spiritually rich, for it is the merciful who are rich in mercy.

It is also the merciful who are rich in truth. Unless we learn the meaning of mercy by exercising it toward others, we never have any real knowledge of what it means to love Christ. Not because our mercy to others teaches us love Christ, directly, but rather because Christ's love in our own lives acts dynamically to reach others *through us,* thereby revealing him to us in our own souls.

Without love and compassion for others, our own apparent "love" for Christ is a fiction.

THOMAS MERTON [24]

Pray constantly. (Epistle)

A man of prayer will do more in a year's apostolate than another in a lifetime.

LOUIS LALLEMANT [25]

37

Lord, it is good to be here. (Gospel)

Three degrees of love I shall tell thee, for I would that thou might win to the highest. The first degree is called *Insuperable,* the second *Inseparable,* the third *Singular.* . . .

The third degree is highest and most wondrous to win. That is called *Singular,* for it has no peer. Singular love is when all comfort and solace are closed out of thy heart, but that of Jesus Christ alone. It seeks no other joy. For the sweetness of him that is in this degree is so comforting and lasting in His love, so burning and gladdening, that he or she who is in this degree may feel the fire of love burning in their souls as well as thou mayest feel thy finger burn if thou dost put it in the fire. But that fire, though it be hot, is so delectable and wonderful that I cannot describe it.

Then thy soul is Jesus-loving, Jesus-thinking, Jesus-desiring, only breathing in the desire of Him, singing to Him, burning for Him, resting in Him. Then the song of praise and love is come. Then thy thought turns to love and melody. Then it behoves thee to *sing* psalms that before thou didst *say.* Then must thou take long over a few psalms. Then wilt thou think death sweeter than honey, for then thou art full certain to see Him whom thou lovest. Then mayest thou boldly say: "I languish for love." Then mayest thou say: "I sleep and my heart watches."

In the first degree men may say: "I languish for love" and "I long for love," and in the other degree also. For languishing is when men faint because of sickness, and they that are in these two degrees fall from all the desires of this world and from the lust and pleasure of sinful life, setting their intent and their hearts to the love of God. Therefore they may say: "I languish for love," and much more they that are in the second degree than in the first. But the soul that is in the third degree is like a burning fire, and as the nightingale that loves song and melody and faints for great love; so that the soul is so much comforted in the praise and loving of God, and till death comes is singing spiritually to Jesus, and in Jesus, and of Jesus, not crying bodily with the mouth, of which manner of singing I do not speak, for both good and bad have that song, and this manner of song nobody has unless he be in the third degree of love. To which degree it is impossible to come but in great plenitude of love.

Therefore if thou wilt know what kind of joy that song has, I tell thee that no man knows but he or she that feels it, that has it, and that praises God therewith. One thing I tell thee: it is of heaven and God gives it to whom He will, but not without great grace coming before. Who has it thinks all the song and all the minstrelsy of earth but sorrow and woe beside it. In sovereign rest shall they be who may gain it. Wanderers and babblers and those who keep visitors early and late, night and day, or any that are entangled with sin silfully and wittingly, or that have delight in any earthly thing, they are as far therefrom as heaven is from earth.

RICHARD ROLLE [26]

SECOND SUNDAY IN LENT

Accidentally or by design, the gospels for the first two Sundays in Lent commemorate the two peak moments in the earthly experience of God Incarnate—the Passion always excepted.

The Temptation and the Transfiguration are a pair of companion pictures. On both occasions, the veil which parts the natural from the supernatural is lifted; on both occasions (if we will allow the evangelists to tell their own story) a demonstration was made, not so much for our Lord's sake as for the sake of those who shared his solitude. In order that the devil might test the strength of this new Champion's armour, our Lord would be seen at his most human, accessible though not attentive to suggestions of evil. In order that the chief apostles might be fortified against the scandal of the Cross, our Lord would be seen in a humanity so glorified that divinity shone through.

And in either case, the manifestation was transitory. *The devil left him for a season*—there was to be no other open trial of his constancy till Gethsemane. *They saw no man any more*—the vision had faded into the less dazzling sunlight. Christ would be the pattern of the Christian life, so far as that was possible, in the experiences he underwent. For him, as for his servants, there should be an alternation; now he would be dragged down, now he would be lifted up, in man's fashion, to prove that he was really man.

For many, perhaps for most, of those who have been conformed, right through, to his likeness, there has been a long apprenticeship of discouragement, when they were assaulted by temptations not felt, or not felt as temptations, by us others. It seemed as if it would last, but did not last, for a lifetime. Afterwards, they were admitted to a sense of the Divine presence, even more beyond our compass. Yet this, too, was transitory; *it is good for us to be here . . .* , yes, but not indefinitely; there must be a return to the multitudes and to the plain. Light and darkness, bless ye the Lord.

RONALD KNOX [27]

This is my beloved Son in whom I am well pleased. Listen to him. (Gospel)

God has now so spoken, that nothing remains unspoken; for that which He partially revealed to the Prophets He has now revealed all in Him, giving unto us all, that is, His Son. And, therefore, he who should now enquire of God in the ancient way, seeking visions or revelations, would offend Him; because he does not fix his eyes upon Christ alone, disregarding all besides. To such an one the answer of God is: *This is My beloved Son, in Whom I am well pleased, hear Him.* [Mt. 17, 5] I have spoken all by My Word, My Son; fix your eyes upon Him, for in Him I have spoken and revealed all, and you will find in Him more than you desire or ask. For if you desire partial visions, revelations, or words, fix your eyes upon Him, and you shall find all. He is My whole Voice and Answer, My whole Vision and Revelation, which I spoke, answered, made, and revealed, when I have Him to be your Brother, Master, Companion, Ransom and Reward. I descended upon Him with My Spirit on Mount Tabor and said, *This is My Beloved Son, in whom I am well pleased, hear Him.* It is not for you now to seek new oracles and responses; for when I spoke in former times it was to promise Christ: and the prayers of those who then enquired of Me were prayers for

40

Christ and expectations of His coming, in whom all good was comprehended, according to the teaching of the Evangelists and Apostles. But, now, he who shall enquire of Me in the ancient way, or hope for an answer at My mouth, or that I should make to him any revelation, shows that he is not content with Christ, and therefore grievously wrongs My Beloved Son. While you have Christ you have nothing to ask of Me, nothing to desire in the way of visions or revelations. Look well unto Him, and you will find that I have given all this and much more in Christ. If you desire a word of consolation from My mouth, behold My Son obedient unto Me and afflicted for My love, and you will see how great is the answer I give you. If you desire to learn of God secret things, fix your eyes upon Christ, and you will find the profoundest mysteries, the wisdom and marvels of God, hidden in Him: *In whom,* says the Apostle, *are hid all the treasures of wisdom and knowledge.* [Col. 2, 3] These treasures will be sweeter and more profitable to you than all those things you desire to know. It was in these that the Apostle gloried when he said, *I judged not myself to know anything among you but Jesus Christ and Him crucified.* [1 Cor. 2, 2] If you desire other visions and revelations, Divine or bodily, look upon His Sacred Humanity, and you will find there more than can ever enter into your thoughts, *for in Him dwells all the fulness of the Godhead corporally.* [Col. 2, 9]

ST. JOHN OF THE CROSS [28]

MONDAY OF THE SECOND WEEK IN LENT

When you have lifted up the Son of Man, then you will know. . . . (Gospel)

Passion and glory are indeed successive not only chronologically but logically inasmuch as the Passion leads to the glorifying of Christ himself (his rising from the dead and his being lifted up to the right hand of the Father), and then that glory is the direct cause of the glory and wonder of Pentecost, the coming down of divine life to humanity. Nevertheless it is our Lord himself who, as the darkness falls upon him and Judas goes out into the darkness, tells the others: *Now is the Son of Man glorified.* [Jn. 13, 31] The tree *is* glory, and for two reasons. First it is the final and complete glorifying of the Father by the Son: *Now is the Son of Man glorified, and God is glorified in him.* [Jn. 13, 31–32] And in that giving of glory Christ himself is, so to speak, fulfilled, for he is (as John would say) the "true Glory": it is the Sun's nature to be radiant, to be glorious but also to give glory. Secondly, the tree is glory because men find life and glory through gazing upon it: *the Son of Man is to be lifted up like the serpent in the wilderness* [Jn. 3, 14], of which the Lord God had said that whosoever gazed upon it should live: *he is to be lifted up in order that those who gaze upon him, in faith, may have the life which is eternal* [Jn. 3, 15] and, as St. Paul tells the Corinthians, *may become transfigured into the likeness of his glory, reflecting it as in a mirror and so borrowing glory from that Glory.* [2 Cor. 3, 18]

GERALD VANN [29]

In its highest and most general sense, the doctrine of the Cross is that to which all men adhere who believe that the vast movement and agitation of human life opens on to a road which leads somewhere, and that that road *climbs upward.* Life has a term: therefore it imposes a particular direction, orientated, in fact, towards the highest possible spiritualisation by means of the greatest possible effort. To admit that group of fundamental principles is already to range oneself among the disciples —distant, perhaps, and implicit, but nevertheless real—of Christ crucified. Once that first choice has been made, the first distinction has been drawn between the brave who will succeed and the pleasure-seekers who will fail, between the elect and the condemned.

This rather vague attitude is clarified and carried further by Christianity. Above all, by revealing an original fall, Christianity provides our intelligence with a reason for the disconcerting excess of sin and suffering at certain points. Next, in order to win our love and secure our faith, it unveils to our eyes and hearts the moving and unfathomable reality of the historical Christ in whom the exemplary life of an individual man conceals this mys-

42

terious drama: the Master of the world, leading, like an element of the world, not only an elemental life, but (in addition to this and because of it) leading the total life of the universe, which he has shouldered and assimilated by experiencing it himself. And finally by the crucifixion and death of this adored being, Christianity signifies to our thirst for happiness that the term of creation is not to be sought in the temporal zones of our visible world, but that the effort required of our fidelity must be consummated *beyond a total transformation* of ourselves and of everything surrounding us.

Thus the perspectives of renunciation implied in the exercise of life itself are gradually expanded. Ultimately we find ourselves thoroughly uprooted, as the Gospel desires, from everything perceptible on earth. But the process of uprooting ourselves has happened little by little and according to a rhythm which has neither alarmed nor wounded the respect we owe to the admirable beauties of the human effort.

It is perfectly true that the Cross means going beyond the frontiers of the sensible world and even, in a sense, breaking with it. The final stages of the ascent to which it calls us compel us to cross a threshold, a critical point, where we lose touch with the zone of the realities of the senses. That final "excess," glimpsed and accepted from the first steps, inevitably puts everything we do in a special light and gives it a particular significance. That is exactly where the folly of Christianity lies in the eyes of the "wise" who are not prepared to stake the good which they now hold in their hands on a total "beyond." But that agonising flight from the experimental zones—which is what the Cross means— is only (as should be strongly emphasised) the sublime aspect of a law common to *all* life. Towards the peaks, shrouded in mist from our human eyes, whither the Cross beckons us, we rise by a path which is the way of universal progress. The royal road of the Cross is no more nor less than the road of human endeavour supernaturally righted and prolonged. Once we have fully grasped the meaning of the Cross, we are no longer in danger of finding life sad and ugly. We shall simply have become more attentive to its barely comprehensible solemnity.

To sum up, Jesus on the Cross is both the symbol and the reality of the immense labour of the centuries which has, little by little, raised up the created spirit and brought it back to the depth of the divine *milieu*. He represents (and in a true sense, he is) creation, as, upheld by God, it reascends the slopes of being, sometimes clinging to things for support, sometimes tearing itself from them in order to pass beyond them, and always compensating, by physical suffering, for the setbacks caused by its moral downfalls.

The Cross is therefore not inhuman but superhuman. We can now understand that from the very first, from the very origins of mankind as we know it, the Cross was placed on the crest of the road which leads to the highest peaks of creation. But, in the growing light of Revelation, its arms, which at first were bare, show themselves to have put on Christ: *Crux inuncta*. At first sight the bleeding body may seem funereal to us. Is it not from the night that it shines forth? But if we go nearer we shall recognise the flaming Seraph of Alverno [Francis of Assisi] whose passion and compassion are *incendium mentis*. The Christian is not asked to swoon in the shadow, but to climb in the light of the Cross.

PIERRE TEILHARD DE CHARDIN [30]

TUESDAY OF THE SECOND WEEK IN LENT

You have only one Master, Christ. (Gospel)

I consider Jesus Christ in all persons and in ourselves: Jesus Christ as a Father in His Father, Jesus Christ as a Brother in His brethren, Jesus Christ as poor in the poor, Jesus Christ as rich in the rich, Jesus Christ as Doctor and Priest in priests, Jesus Christ as Sovereign in princes, etc. For by His glory He is all that is great, being God; and by His mortal life He is all that is poor and abject. Therefore He has taken this unhappy condition, so that He could be in all persons, and the model of all conditions.

BLAISE PASCAL [31]

He who humbles himself will be exalted. (Gospel)

When we abolish humility, remorse, and repentance from our lives, we deceive ourselves; we live in a fake perfection; we abandon holiness and integration because we leave out the awareness of the demonic, egotistic inclinations which are as much a part of our fallen nature as our more virtuous, godly tendencies. Our shadow is always with us. And our shadow is more clear and sharp-edged when we walk in the fullness of the sun. The person who grows in the light of grace sees more clearly the darkness of sin. The infinity of light makes him more aware of the abyss of darkness. The saint is the man who walks constantly between two abysses. No one speaks so eloquently as he of the love and grace of God, and no one laments so poignantly the power of the demonic in his life. Humility and repentance prevent the blind repression of our awareness of those modes of existence which are incompatible with our life project. If we unfortunately repress the awareness of the growth of these modes of life, they will burst forth in dreams and neurotic symptoms; they will generate a conflict between themselves and our conscious plan of life.

ADRIAN VAN KAAM [32]

WEDNESDAY OF THE SECOND WEEK IN LENT

The Son of Man will be mocked and scourged and crucified. . . . Can you drink of the cup of which I am about to drink? (Gospel)

Do you hope to escape what no mortal man has ever yet escaped? What saint in this world has been without his cross and without some trouble? Truly, our Lord Jesus was not one hour without some sorrow and pain as long as He lived here. It behooved Him to suffer death and to rise again and so to enter into His glory. How is it, then, that you seek any other way to heaven than this plain, high way of the Cross. All the life of Christ

45

was Cross and martyrdom; do you seek pleasure and joy? You err greatly if you seek any other thing than to suffer, for all this mortal life is full of misery and is all surrounded and marked with crosses. And the more highly a man profits in spirit, the more painful crosses will he find, for, by the firm certainty of Christ's love, in which he daily increases, the pain of this exile daily appears to him more and more.

Nevertheless, a man vexed with pain is not left wholly without all comfort, for he sees well that great fruit and high reward shall grow unto him by the bearing of his cross. And when a man freely submits himself to such tribulation, then all the burden of tribulation is suddenly turned into a great trust of heavenly solace. The more the flesh is punished by tribulation, the more the soul is daily strengthened by inward consolation. And sometimes the soul will feel such comforts in adversities, that for love and a desire to be conformed to Christ Crucified, it would not be without sorrow and trouble. The more it may suffer for His love here, the more acceptable it will be to him in the life to come. But this working is not in the power of man, save through the grace of God—that is to say, that a frail man should accept and love adversities that his natural inclinations so much abhor and flee.

It is not in the power of man gladly to bear the Cross, to love the Cross, to chastise the body and make it submissive to the will of the spirit, to flee honors gladly, to sustain reproofs, to despise himself and to desire to be despised, patiently to suffer adversities with all the displeasures that accompany them, and not to desire any manner of profit in this world. If you trust in yourself, you will never bring all this about. But if you trust in God, He will send you strength from heaven, and the world and the flesh will be made subject to you. Yes, and if you are strongly armed with faith, and are marked with the Cross of Christ as His family servant, you will not need to fear your spiritual enemy, for he will also be made subject to you, so that he will have no power against you. Steel yourself as a faithful servant of God manfully to bear the Cross of your Lord Jesus Who, for your love, was crucified upon the Cross. Prepare yourself to suffer all manner of adversities and inconveniences in this wretched life, for so it will be with you wherever you hide

46

yourself. There is no remedy for escaping, but you must always keep yourself in patience. If you desire to be a dear and well-beloved friend of Christ, drink effectively with Him a draft of the chalice of His tribulation. As for consolations, commit them to His will so that He may ordain them as He knows most expedient for you. But as for yourself, as much as lies in your power, dispose yourself to suffer, and when tribulations come, take them as special consolations.

THOMAS A KEMPIS [33]

THURSDAY OF THE SECOND WEEK IN LENT

I, the Lord, alone probe the mind and the test the heart. (Epistle)

We have a strange illusion that mere time cancels sin. I have heard others, and I have heard myself, recounting cruelties and falsehoods committed in boyhood as if they were no concern of the present speaker's, and even with laughter. But mere time does nothing either to the fact or to the guilt of a sin. The guilt is washed out not by time but by repentance and the blood of Christ: if we have repented these early sins we should remember the price of our forgiveness and be humble. As for the fact of a sin, is it probable that anything cancels it? All times are eternally present to God. Is it not at least possible that along some one line of His multi-dimensional eternity He sees you forever in the nursery pulling the wings off a fly, forever toadying, lying, and lusting as a schoolboy, forever in that moment of cowardice or insolence as a subaltern? It may be that salvation consists not in the cancelling of these eternal moments but in the perfected humility that bears the shame forever, rejoicing in the occasion which it furnished to God's compassion and glad that it should be common knowledge to the universe.

C. S. LEWIS [34]

I am tormented in this flame. (Gospel)

And what have you laymen made of hell? A kind of penal servitude for eternity, on the lines of your convict prisons on earth, to which you condemn in advance all the wretched felons your police have hunted from the beginning—"enemies of society," as you call them. You're kind enough to include the blasphemers and the profane. What proud or reasonable man could stomach such a notion of God's justice? And when you find that notion inconvenient, it's easy enough for you to put it on one side. Hell is judged by the standards of the world, and hell is not of this world, it is of the other world, and still less of this Christian society. An eternal expiation—! The miracle is that we on earth were ever able to think of such a thing, when scarcely has our sin gone out of us, and one look, a sign, a dumb appeal suffices for grace and pardon to swoop down, as an eagle from topmost skies. It's because the lowest of human beings, even though he no longer thinks he can love, still has in him the power of loving. Our very hate is resplendent, and the least tormented of the fiends would warm himself in what we call our despair, as in a morning of glittering sunshine. Hell is not to love any more, madame. Not to love any more! That sounds quite ordinary to you. To a human being still alive, it means to love less or love elsewhere. To understand is still a way of loving. But suppose this faculty which seems so inseparably ours, of our very essence, should disappear! Oh, prodigy! To stop loving, to stop understanding—and yet to live. The error common to us all is to invest these damned with something still inherently alive, something of our own inherent mobility, whereas in truth time and movement have ceased for them; they are fixed for ever. Alas, if God's own hand were to lead us to one of these unhappy *things,* even if once it had been the dearest of our friends, what could we say to it? Truly, if one of us, if a living man, the vilest, most contemptible of the living, were cast into those burning depths, I should still be ready to share his suffering, I would claim him from his executioner. . . . To share his suffering! The sorrow, the unutterable loss of those charred stones which once were men, is that they have nothing more to be shared. . . .

There's a time for mercy and a time for justice, and the only final grief is one day to stand impenitent under Merciful Eyes.

GEORGES BERNANOS [35]

FRIDAY OF THE SECOND WEEK IN LENT

This is the heir. Come, let us kill him. (Gospel)

This parable may be said to be the last great appeal of Jesus to the priests and elders, the Scribes and Pharisees. It is the summing up of His indictment, the collecting of all the evidence before the sentence is finally pronounced. For His theme He does not go far afield; as He has always done with others, so with these men He chooses an illustration which was familiar to them all. They were, or they claimed to be, familiar with the Scriptures; from the first the chosen people had been likened to a vineyard. . . .

This His vine the Lord had entrusted to His husbandmen; to Moses and the Judges; to the kings; but most of all to the priests and Levites, the Scribes and the Pharisees, the lawyers and the ancients, the keepers of the Law and its interpreters. Since the day when the Law had come into their hands, it had been for them to administer it, to cultivate the vineyard of the Lord. And with what result had this been done? As before the eye of Jesus had looked across all space, so now it looked through all time. It went back to the warnings of Moses before he died, who feared so much lest his own might again one day hanker for the flesh-pots of Egypt. It looked to those first corruptions witnessed to in the Book of Judges, when the Canaanites were spared to the ruin of Israel, when idolatry spread throughout the land. It looked upon the days of the Kings, when again the people fell, led on by their rulers, and the prophets came, and appealed, and wept for Israel, and were ignored or persecuted or put to death. . . .

He looked at the destruction of Israel and Juda, the Captivity and the Restoration; and yet again what could He see but a further hardening of heart, a further concentration on them-

49

selves, a further building up of their own conception of the Messias that was to come? Thus they had gone on from generation to generation refusing to learn from those were outside themselves, until to receive the herald of the Kingdom had become wellnigh impossible. . . .

And yet there had been the other side; the patience and long-suffering of His Father. How He had borne with them! If the story of His chosen people had been one of continued infidelities, likewise had it been one of continued mercies. . . .

> *O the Lord*
> *The Lord God*
> *Merciful and gracious*
> *Patient and of much compassion*
> *And true*
> *Who keepeth mercy unto thousands*
> *Who takest away iniquity and wickedness and sin*
> *And no man of himself is innocent before thee.*
>
> [EX. 34, 6–7]

With passages such as these their whole record rang; invitation, acceptance, rejection, punishment, repentance, reconciliation, restoration, —from the beginning the whole history of His Father's dealings with His own had been consistently the same, no matter how low they had sunk. . . . and in describing the Father He describes Himself. In the midst of this day of cruel cunning on the part of His enemies, in the midst of the vehement denunciation, rising more and more as the day goes on, He has only the heart for forgiveness, if only they will be forgiven. After what He has said of the doing of these husbandmen, their insults, their murders, their contempt of their lord; after we have been compelled to think of the wrath they have incurred, the pathos of the picture comes upon us almost with a shock:

> *Then the lord of the vineyard*
> *Having yet one son*
> *Most dear to him*
> *Also sent him unto them last of all*

Saying: What shall I do?
I will send my beloved son
It may be when they see him
They will reverence him.

"It may be"; it was by no means sure. The lord will risk the life of his own son that he might find some means of reconciliation with these hired men.

In this way, on this note, does Jesus swing the story from the past into the present, and from the present into the future. In four days more all will be over. Vividly for the last time He puts before them the folly as well as the iniquity of the deed they contemplate; could patience, endurance, love itself, go further?

Whom when the husbandmen saw
They thought within themselves
Saying one to another
This is the heir
Come let us kill him
And the inheritance shall be ours
And laying hold on him
They killed him
And cast him out of the vineyard.

And now once more we see the overwhelming irony which would at times appear in His dealings with His enemies. The tale they would understand; the justice of retribution on those husbandmen they would not deny; but the application to themselves in their blindness of heart they would fail to recognize. Instead they would look about them. They would see the vineyard of the Lord, the Jewish people, worked by a race of foreign husbandmen, Pontius Pilate and his Romans. They would rejoice to think that thus cleverly this Jesus of Nazareth had proved the injustice of the Roman tyranny. While they so interpret His words in their hearts He turns to them and asks:

When therefore the lord of the vineyard shall come
What will he do to those husbandmen?

51

and at once they answer:

> *He will bring those men to an evil end*
> *And will let out his vineyard to other husbandmen*
> *That they shall render him the fruit in due season.*

Jesus stood and looked at them; they had pronounced their own condemnation. Like Esther with Aman, like Nathan before David, He had only now to say:

> *Thou art the man!*

For a moment He paused. Then pointing to them, with that steadiness of countenance which they had seen so often, and which needed no further argument, He repeated what they had said:

> *He will come*
> *And will destroy those husbandmen*
> *And will give the vineyard to others.*

At once it dawned upon them what they had done. It was not the Romans but themselves that were guilty; not the Romans but themselves were destined to be rejected. Before they could recover from their stupor they cried:

> *God forbid!*

They would reverse their decision, but it was too late.

ALBAN GOODIER [36]

SATURDAY OF THE SECOND WEEK IN LENT

While he was still a long way off his father was moved with compassion. (Gospel)

You are to be perfect, as your heavenly Father is perfect: such is the veritable commandment we find in the Gospel [Mt. 5, 48], an echo in fact of the one in the Old Testament: *You shall be holy: for I the Lord your God am holy.* [Lv. 19, 2] And we of course know very well that God has a sort of ascendancy over our lives; we know very well that we shall really have to become holy in his eyes—either in this world or after death, through the final purifications of Purgatory—so that everything may turn out well for us, if I may put it in such familiar terms. But, coming down to the immediate, practical side of things here, what does this call to share in the perfection of God, holy, increate and pure spirit, signify; what are we to take it to mean here and now? Well, Jesus already answered the question when he said to Philip: *Whoever has seen me, has seen the Father* [Jn. 14, 9], and he is consequently so completely "the way" that we cannot tend towards the perfection that God demands of us without becoming like him.

In other words, to imitate the Father we must imitate Jesus, as he is the Image of the Father and the Father's eternal Word, humanly expressed. Jesus is the revelation of the Father in its plenitude, and at the same time that revelation is given, in him, its human plenitude, since, as St. Paul says: *In Christ the whole plenitude of Deity is embodied.* [Col. 2, 9] Not only does Jesus speak to us of God as no prophet had done before him; he also manifests the Father to us by everything he is and everything he does. Take, for instance, that parable which you all know so well —the parable of the prodigal son. Jesus tells us here that *while he was still a long way off, his father saw him . . . and, running up, he threw his arms round his neck and kissed him.* [Lk. 15, 20] But Jesus has told us much more about God's merciful love through his own behaviour towards sinners and his death on the Cross.

We ourselves know how impossible it is to make known, really and completely, with words, someone whom we love. We may describe the person to the best of our ability; we may show all the photographs of him that we like, but we cannot get across that something which makes of each man a unique being, that something which can only be transmitted at all by the sight of him, by his actions, by a look meeting his, or through sharing in his life and concerns. As a matter of fact, you must admit that knowing someone is an affair that has no end to it, and when the "someone" is God himself, what are you going to say? If, then, we want to know God as he is in his mystery, it will not be enough for us to listen to what Jesus has told us about him, nor yet to search into the life of Jesus and discover there God's visage and God's heart; we must follow Jesus more closely still than that and, imitating his life, model our own lives upon the visage and the heart of God.

RENE VOILLAUME [37]

What magnificent parables Christ found to make us understand the mercy with which His heart overflowed and which is but the pouring forth of the mercy of the Father: the prodigal son, the groat found again, the lost sheep, all these in the XVth chapter of St. Luke, in which, in face of the recriminations of the Pharisees, Our Lord justifies His attitude toward the sinner. What these parables emphasize is not the joy of the pardoned sinner, as we might expect from our human point of view, but rather the joy of God at the return of the sinners: the father of the prodigal son, the woman who finds her groat, the shepherd who brings back his sheep. God can receive nothing from the human race, which, being nothing by its nature, has rendered itself still more vile by its sin; but the human race has become precious for Him because He loves it. It is precious for Him like a piece of silver for a poor woman, like sheep for the shepherd, like a son to his father. That is the explanation of the magnificent history of salvation, of the existence of the organ of salvation, the Church. It all comes from the fact that the Father desires the return of lost humanity to the fold. And this explains the desire which quickens Christ and which lives in the Church. It is with this desire that we should permeate ourselves if we want to have a spiritual apostolate. Perhaps we now see more clearly that the apostolic desire is not something which has its source and root in us. It does not consist in directing our natural need for activity toward a higher goal, nor in our tendency to bring others to share our ideas. Rather, it is the merciful initiative of the Father come down into our hearts. It is His eternal love for sinful humanity which has taken possession of us. But it is a treasure we carry in fragile vases. It is the appearance of the highest and most saintly in our narrow, mean, egoistic, impure hearts.

YVES DE MONTCHEUIL [38]

THIRD SUNDAY IN LENT

Live in love. (Epistle)

How very difficult it is for the human soul not to love something. Of necessity our minds and wills must be drawn to some kind of affection. Carnal love is overcome by spiritual love. Desire is extinguished by a deeper desire. Whatever is taken from carnal love is given to the higher love. Therefore, as you lie on your bed, murmur this over and over again, *On my bed at night I have sought Him Whom my soul adores.* [Ct. 3, 1]

ST. JEROME [39]

Christ loved us and delivered himself up for us. (Epistle)

God's patience is His patience with me. And I to some extent am able to judge what that means. I can judge because I know how difficult it is to be patient with myself. It nearly drives me mad having to bear with myself. Doctors say that it can make man ill and that many mental diseases are caused because man comes to the point where he cannot endure himself any longer and tries to escape from himself by feigning another personality. Often the disease goes even further. It can lead to physical suffering—a curious expiation which man accepts because he cannot overcome the spiritual trouble. Unless we delude ourselves, or have succeeded in reconciling ourselves to our own paltry and petty world, we all know this kind of suffering even though it may not have actually made us ill, and, anyway, where is the border line between health and sickness? We all know the misery, the bitter sterility, when day after day and year after year passes and things never change. One tries for so long to overcome this situation but

55

it refuses to yield. One appears to have overcome it for a time perhaps and then it suddenly returns. And sometimes it seems as though after wearing oneself out trying to overcome it, seven demons have taken the place of the original one.

If God's attitude to us is the same as our own attitude to ourselves, then the outlook is black indeed. If God takes as poor a view of me as I do myself, if God does not bear with my bungling, my dishonesty, my constant failures with greater patience than I do myself, then I am bound to give up in despair. But God is love. And in Him my nature is truer than in myself. In me it is corrupt; in Him it is pure. In His most holy patience He holds in His love my nature which I myself disfigure so terribly and squander so thoughtlessly. From this loving patience He sees and bears me. He has infinite confidence in me. He believes that I am capable of making progress.

ROMANO GUARDINI [40]

Once you were darkness, now you are light. (Epistle)

The mystery of the cross is a mystery of obedience and of love, of which the glorious resurrection is the outcome rather than the recompense. A theme of the entire New Testament is that the death of Christ is an expression of love. It is *the life given as a ransom for the lives of many.* [Mt. 20, 28] Paul tells us: *Order your lives in charity, upon the model of that charity which Christ showed to us, when he gave himself up on our behalf.* [Eph. 5, 2]

As the victim of the holocaust, changed into the immaterial smoke, rose towards God, so Christ, by this act of love and obedience in his voluntary death, returns effectively to his Father. For Paul, then, the redemptive mystery is truly a sacrifice. But the sacrifice of Christ is unique in that *he offers himself.* His sacrifice is identical with his return to the Father, and in him we all return to the Father, He gave himself less in place of men than on our behalf, for our sakes; he performed the greatest act of love that man can accomplish, not to dispense us from loving, but to permit us to love. St. Paul's whole doctrine of the redemption can be summed up by saying that he united the idea of Christ's giving himself to free us from sin to that of our reunion with God.

Christ's return to God and humanity's return in Christ cannot be conceived apart from his glorification, which includes both his resurrection and his ascension. It is because Jesus was raised from the dead that *he has delivered us from the wrath to come.* [1 Th. 1, 10] *If Christ has not risen, vain is your faith, for you are still in your sins.* [1 Cor. 15, 17] It is through the resurrection that Christ has become "the life-giving spirit," giving life to humanity.

Christ communicates this new life to all who participate in his act of obedience and love through faith and baptism. Through baptism, the configuration to the death and resurrection of Christ, we attain a state of justice. Since it is the work of Christ, that state is final in itself. In it we are united to Christ in his death and in his risen life. If we do not fall again into the grips of sin, we will some day attain life in all its fullness.

STANISLAS LYONNET [41]

MONDAY OF THE THIRD WEEK IN LENT

Naaman the Syrian was scandalized by the prophet's plan for his cure. The simplicity of the divine plan for our salvation often shocks us too. Only obedience brings cleansing and insight.

We simple "men-in-the-street" are quite sure that we can love God as much as he wants us to love him.

We do not think that love is something brilliant but something consuming and that doing great actions for God makes us love him less than doing very little things in union with him and as he would have them done.

Besides, we don't really understand the proportions of our actions very well. All we know is that, first, anything we do is bound to be small and, secondly, that anything that God does is bound to be great. These considerations cause us to take a rather quiet view of action.

We know that our whole duty consists in striving for the grace to avoid frantic behavior, in not being fussily selective about what there is to be done, and in understanding that it is God who will act for us. . . .

Each action thus docilely performed causes us both to receive God and to give him fully and in great liberty of spirit to others. *Then life becomes one long feastday*. Each little action is an immense event in which Paradise is delivered to us and in which we can give Paradise to others.

What we are called upon to do is of small import indeed: sweep a floor or hold a pen, speak or keep silent, mend socks or give a lecture, care for the sick or type.

Any activity is just the outer bark of the splendid reality of our encounter with God, an encounter which is renewed at each moment, grows in grace each moment, and which makes a person even more pleasing in the sight of God.

The doorbell is ringing; answer it quickly: it is God coming to love us.

Someone makes inquiries of us; answer him: it is God coming to love us.

It is time to eat; then let us set to: it is God coming to love us.

Let him have his way.

MADELEINE DELBREL [42]

Do little things as though they were great, because of the majesty of Jesus Christ who does them in us, and who lives our life; and do the greatest things as though they were little and easy, because of His omnipotence.

BLAISE PASCAL [43]

Troubled soul, thou art not bound to feel but thou art bound to arise. God loves thee whether thou feelest or not. Thou canst not love when thou wilt, but thou art bound to fight the hatred in thee to the last. Try not to feel good when thou art not good, but cry to Him who is good. He changes not because thou changest. Nay, He has an especial tenderness of love towards thee for that thou art in the dark and hast no light, and His heart is glad when thou dost arise and say, "I will go to my Father." . . . Fold the arms of thy faith, and wait in the quietness until

58

light goes up in thy darkness. Fold the arms of thy Faith I say, but not of thy Action: bethink thee of something that thou oughtest to do, and go to do it, if it be but the sweeping of a room, or the preparing of a meal, or a visit to a friend. Heed not thy feelings: Do thy work.

GEORGE MACDONALD [44]

TUESDAY OF THE THIRD WEEK IN LENT

Where two or three have gathered in my name, I am there among them. (Gospel)

Before the whole world let all Christians confess their faith in God, one and three in the incarnate Son of God, our Redeemer and Lord. United in their efforts, and with mutual respect, let them bear witness to our common hope which does not play us false. In these days when cooperation in social matters is so widespread, all men without exception are called to work together, with much greater reason all those who believe in God, but most of all, all Christians in that they bear the name of Christ. Cooperation among Christians vividly expresses the relationship which in fact already unites them, and it sets in clearer relief the features of Christ the Servant. Such cooperation, which has already begun in many countries, should be developed more and more, particularly in regions where a social and technical evolution is taking place. It should contribute to a just evaluation of the dignity of the human person, to the establishment of the blessings of peace, the application of Gospel principles to social life, and the advancement of the arts and sciences in a truly Christian spirit. Cooperation among Christians should also employ every possible means to relieve the afflictions of our times such as famine and natural disasters, illiteracy and poverty, lack of housing and the unequal distribution of wealth. All believers in Christ can, through such cooperation, be led to acquire a better knowledge and appreciation of one another, and so is made smooth the road which leads to the unity of Christians.

DECREE ON ECUMENISM [45]

Since the renewal of the Churches is an essential part of the movement for Christian unity, the Churches engaged in ecumenism do not strive after an ideal in history but strain after a full fulfillment that even a single visible Church on earth embracing all Christians could not supply. They reach out toward the heavenly Jerusalem. By engaging herself, therefore, in the ecumenical movement a Church, any Church, becomes more conscious of her pilgrim state and yearns more ardently for the day of Christ's return, and anticipating God's judgment in repentance and God's mercy in eschatological hope, she becomes more truly Church.

GREGORY BAUM [46]

WEDNESDAY OF THE THIRD WEEK IN LENT

This people pays me lip service, but their heart is far from me. (Gospel)

No arguments can prevail against the plain fact that Christ, repeatedly and in unmistakable terms, turned away from those who cried "Lord! Lord!" but who did not do his bidding: his bidding that we be crucified with him. A fact which would drive us to despair, were it not that each one of us is more crucified than he knows. If you seek in each man for the cross which is part of his destiny, you will always end by finding it. In each of us, a cross grows as we grow, and to be stretched on it before our last breath, either voluntarily or by force, means salvation.

FRANCOIS MAURIAC [47]

Why do you violate the commandment of God on account of your tradition. (Gospel)

In order to act as Christians, we must first of all act as men. And this is not without importance. Doubtless, a perfect Christian will necessarily fulfil his duties as man, for the law of the Gospel comprises and perfects the natural law. But one meets with Christians, or rather with some calling themselves Christians, and

60

that not only among the simple faithful, but even among religious and priests, who are exact even to scrupulosity as to their self-chosen practices of piety, and yet hold certain precepts of the natural law very cheaply. These people have it at heart not to miss their exercises of devotion, and this is excellent, but, for example, they do not refrain from attacking a neighbour's reputation, from telling falsehoods, and failing to keep their word; they do not scruple to give a wrong meaning to what an author has written nor to infringe the laws of literary or artistic property; they defer, sometimes to the detriment of justice, the payment of their debts, and are not exact in observing the clauses of a contract.

Such as these "whose religion spoils their morality," to use the expression of the great English statesman, Gladstone, have not understood St. Paul's precept: *Veritatem facientes.* There is a want of logic in their spiritual life, there is "untruth." Many of these souls may be unconscious of this "untruth," but it is none the less hurtful, for God does not find in them that order which He wills should reign in all His works.

So then, we must be "true." That is the basis on which grace works. As you know, grace does not destroy nature. Although, by Divine adoption, we have received that which is like a new being, *Nova creatura,* grace (which must become within us the source and principle of new and supernatural operations) presupposes nature and the operations proceeding from it. Far from being opposed to one another, grace and nature, as regards what is good and pure in the latter, are in harmony, each preserving its own character and beauty.

COLUMBA MARMION [48]

THURSDAY OF THE THIRD WEEK IN LENT

I must proclaim the kingdom of God, for this is why I have been sent. (Gospel)

In the days of His earthly ministry Jesus proclaimed the kingdom of God to men. And the meaning of His preaching and His works

61

was this: that His coming is also the beginning of this kingdom, that the Son of God has come to reveal the kingdom to men and bestow it upon them. Although they have been torn away from God by sin, have been subject to evil and death, and have lost their true life, through faith in Christ men may again come to know the one true God and His love for the world; in union with Him they may inherit the new, eternal life for which they were created. Jesus taught that the world does not accept the kingdom of God, because the world *lieth in evil* and has loved the darkness more than the light. The Son of God, therefore, has brought to men not only true doctrine and knowledge of the kingdom, but also salvation. He has conquered evil and sin, which ruled over mankind.

By His whole life He showed us the type of the perfect man, that is, of a man utterly obedient to God. The authority and power by which He forgave sins, healed the sick, and raised the dead existed only through this love and obedience. In His own Person He revealed the kingdom as complete union with God, as the power of love and sacrifice for God and men. He was delivered up to a shameful death and abandoned by all, yet remained the image incarnate of complete self-surrender, perfect love, and absolute humility. By this surrender of self, love has triumphed over hate, and life has conquered death, for God raised Christ from the dead. The evil of the world and the forces of disintegration that rule it have proved powerless, and in one Man they have been overcome. In one Man the kingdom of God —of love, goodness, and eternal life—has penetrated the realm of sin and death.

ALEXANDER SCHMEMANN [49]

The eyes of all look hopefully to you, O Lord. (Gradual)

The virtue of hope does not foster a complacent egoism. The solidarity of our salvation with the fulfillment of the hopes and expectations of all creation broadens our perspectives. Although God expects a full measure of personal cooperation with His freely bestowed gifts and graces, He likewise counts on our share in the work towards the salvation of the whole world. Our united efforts towards the establishment of peace and order are the most appropriate expressions of Christian hope and the surest means of salvation for our weaker brethren.

Our hope is directed to the eternal kingdom of charity. We shall reach our destiny only in the true solidarity of hope, for salvation is promised to those who in true concern and charity for others bear witness to God's supreme power.

BERNARD HARING [50]

FRIDAY OF THE THIRD WEEK IN LENT

Jesus came to a town of Samaria called Sichar. (Gospel)

This Gospel is the culminating point in the moral preaching of Jesus. There is something new in the world, when Jesus says to a sinful woman this unsurpassable word, *God is a spirit.* The highest moral revelation was made, at the well of Jacob, to this woman to whom Jesus had just uncovered her sins. It is evident that, having heard this voice, she would sin no more.

God is a spirit. Yet he seeks men who will adore him. Therefore, man is also a spirit. He has a wonderful dignity. The whole value of life lies in this; and the value of man lies not in what he does, but in what he is.

We have only to listen to these words of Jesus to the Samaritan woman to realize that never has religion been raised to such heights. When one believes in this religion, all pharisaism is abolished. There is no more "religion of works." What God asks for is the gift of our spirit, because he himself is spirit.

We are present here at the founding of the "Religion of the spirit"; *Never did man speak like this man.* [Jn. 7, 46]

Even the agents of the high priests and the Pharisees were disarmed by the words of Jesus, and, twenty centuries later, we experience the same emotion.

"Lord, it is not because I have been told that you are the Son of God that I listen to your Word, but because your Word is

63

beautiful beyond all human word. And it is by that that I recognize that you are the Son of God" (André Gide).

MAURICE ZUNDEL [51]

> Let us meditate on the Gospels.
> Amidst the confusion
> of so many human words,
> the Gospel
> is the only voice
> that enlightens and attracts,
> that consoles and quenches thirst.

JOHN XXIII [52]

SATURDAY OF THE THIRD WEEK IN LENT

Let him who is without sin among you be the first to cast a stone. (Gospel)

There was once a brother exceeding careful about seeking goodness. And being sore troubled by the demon of lust, he came to an old man and told him his thoughts. The old man was inexperienced: and when he heard, he was indignant, and said he was a wicked brother, unworthy of his monk's habit, because he conceived thoughts like that. When the brother heard this, he despaired of himself, and left his cell, and started on his way back to the world. But by God's providence, Abba Apollos met him. And seeing him disturbed and melancholy he asked him: "Son, why are you so sad?" The brother, much embarrassed, at first said not a word. But when the old man pressed him to say what was happening to him, he confessed, and said: "It is because lustful thoughts trouble me. I confessed them to that old man, and he says I now have no hope of salvation. So I am desperate at myself, and am on my way back to the world." When Father Apollos heard this, he went on asking questions like a wise doctor, and advised him thus: "Do not be cast down, son, nor despair of yourself. Even at my age and experience of the spiritual life, I am still sorely troubled by thoughts like yours. Do not fail at this point, because this trouble cannot be cured by our efforts, but only by God's mercy. Grant me what I ask, just today, and go back to your cell."

The brother obeyed him. But Abba Apollos went away to the cell of the old man who had made him desperate. He stood outside the cell, and prayed the Lord with tears, and said: "Lord, who allowest men to be tempted for their good, transfer the war which that brother is suffering to this old man: let him learn by experience in his old age what many years have not taught him, and so let him find out how to sympathize with people undergoing this kind of temptation." And as soon as he ended his prayer, he saw a negro standing by the cell firing arrows at the old man. As though stricken, he began to totter and lurch like a drunken man. And when he could bear it no longer, he came out of his cell, and set out on the same road by which the young man started to return to the world. Abba Apollos understood what had happened, and met him. He approached him, and said: "Where are you going? And why are you so troubled within?" The old man, seeing that the holy Apollos understood what had happened, was ashamed and said nothing. But Abba Apollos said to him: "Return to your cell, and see your own weakness in another, and keep your own heart. For either you were ignorant of the devil in spite of your age, or you were contemptuous, and did not deserve to struggle for strength with the devil as all other men must. But *struggle* is not the right word, when you could not stand up to his attack for one day. This has happened to you because of the young man. He came to you because he was being attacked by the common enemy of us all. You ought to have given him words of consolation to help him against the devil's attack. But instead you drove him to despair. You did not remember the wise man's saying, whereby we are ordered to deliver the men who are drawn towards death, and not forbear to redeem men ready to be killed. You did not remember our Saviour's parable: *You should not break the bruised reed, nor quench the smoking flax.* [Mt. 12, 20] Not a single person could endure the enemy's clever attack, nor quench, nor control the leaping fire natural to the body, unless God's grace preserved us in our weakness. In all our prayers we should pray for his grace to save us, so that he may turn aside the scourge aimed even at

65

you. For he makes a man to grieve, and then lifts him up to salvation: he strikes, and his hand heals: he humbles and exalts, mortifies and enlivens: leads to hell and brings back from hell."

So saying, Abba Apollos prayed again, and at once the old man was freed from his inner war. Abba Apollos urged him to ask God to give him the tongue of the learned, to know the time when it is best to speak.

SAYINGS OF THE FATHERS [53]

FOURTH SUNDAY IN LENT

You are children of the promise. (Epistle)

Christ is the Light of nations. Because this is so, this Sacred Synod gathered together in the Holy Spirit eagerly desires, by proclaiming the Gospel to every creature, to bring the light of Christ to all men, a light brightly visible on the countenance of the Church. Since the Church is in Christ like a Sacrament or as a sign and instrument both of a very closely knit union with God and of the unity of the whole human race, it desires now to unfold more fully to the faithful of the Church and to the whole world its own inner nature and universal mission. This it intends to do following faithfully the teaching of previous Councils. The present-day conditions of the world add great urgency to this work of the Council so that all men, joined more closely today by various social, technical, and cultural ties, might also attain fuller unity in Christ.

DOGMATIC CONSTITUTION ON THE CHURCH [54]

If a man of the Church of the future were to read the Vatican II Constitution on the Church, what would he pick out as particularly striking? What would he read as an almost prophetic voice to him out of the past? . . . One of the first things that would come home to our imagined Christian of the future would be the statement that the Church is the sacrament of salvation of the *world*. That is found in the very Introduction to the Decree. Our imagined Christian will be living as a member of the little flock in an immeasurably vast world of non-Christians. How in such circumstances is he to think of his Church? How is he still to live with the inalienable consciousness that the Church is founded by God, by Christ, the Lord of all history, that it is the sole eternally valid religion? How is he to do so, when the day when all mankind will be Christian will seem to him unimaginably more distant than it is even for us, because no force of a homogeneous society and tradition will operate any longer in favor of the Church?

He will be able to do it only if he views the Church as the sacrament of the world's salvation.

KARL RAHNER [55]

Jesus took the loaves, gave thanks, and distributed them. (Gospel) *In John's Gospel there are several details in this account which will remind the Christian reader of the Eucharist. It is a prelude to Jesus' lengthy discourse on the bread of life in both word and sacrament.*

At the Last Supper, on the night when he was betrayed, our Savior instituted the eucharistic sacrifice of his body and blood. He did this in order to perpetuate the sacrifice of the Cross throughout the centuries until he should come again, and so to entrust to his beloved spouse, the Church, a memorial of his death and resurrection: a sacrament of love, a sign of unity, a bond of charity, a paschal banquet in which Christ is eaten, the mind is filled with grace, and a pledge of future glory is given to us.

The Church, therefore, earnestly desires that Christ's faithful, when present at this mystery of faith, should not be there as strangers or silent spectators; on the contrary, through a good understanding of the rites and prayers they should take part in the sacred action conscious of what they are doing, with devotion and full collaboration. They should be instructed by God's word and be nourished at the table of the Lord's body; they should give thanks to God; by offering the immaculate victim, not only through the hands of the priest, but also with him, they should learn also to offer themselves; through Christ the Media-

67

tor, they should be drawn day by day into ever more perfect union with God and with each other, so that finally God may be all in all.

CONSTITUTION ON THE SACRED LITURGY [56]

MONDAY OF THE FOURTH WEEK IN LENT

Zeal for your house has eaten me up. (Gospel)

He enters into the Court of the Gentiles, the most spacious and most densely crowded of all. The great, sunny, well-paved terrace is not the atrium of a sanctuary, but a dirty market-place. An immense, roaring din rises up from the vermin-like crowd of bankers, of buyers and sellers, of money-changers who give and take money. There are herdsmen with their oxen and their flocks of sheep; venders of pigeons and turtle doves, standing by the long lines of their coops; bird-sellers, with cages of chirping sparrows; benches for money-changers, with bowls overflowing with copper and silver. Merchants, their feet in the fresh-dropped dung, handle the flanks of the animals destined for sacrifice; or call with monotonous iteration women who have come there after childbirth, pilgrims who have come to offer a rich sacrifice, lepers who offer living birds for their cure, obtained or hoped for. Money-changers, with a coin hung at their ears as a mark of their trade, gloatingly plunge their greedy talons into gleaming piles; the go-betweens run about in the swarm of the gossiping groups; niggardly, wary provincials hold excited conferences before loosening the purse strings to change their cash for a votive offering, and from time to time a restless ox drowns out with his deep bellow the thin bleating of the lambs, the shrill voices of the women, the clinking of drachma and shekels.

Christ was familiar with the spectacle. He knew that the house of God had been turned into the house of Mammon, and that, instead of silently invoking the Spirit, material-minded men trafficked there in the filth of the Demon, with the priests as their accomplices.

GIOVANNI PAPINI [57]

Jesus found in the temple, which is said to be the house of the Father of the Saviour, that is, in the church or in the preaching of the ecclesiastical and sound word, some who were making His Father's house a house of merchandise. And at all times Jesus finds some of this sort in the temple. For in that which is called the church, which is the house of the living God, the pillar and ground of the truth, when are there not some money-changers sitting who need the strokes of the scourge Jesus made of small cords, and dealers in small coin who require to have their money poured out and their tables overturned? When are there not those who are inclined to merchandise, but need to be held to the plough and the oxen, that having put their hand to it and not turning round to the things behind them, they may be fit for the kingdom of God? When are there not those who prefer the mammon of unrighteousness to the sheep which give them the material for their true adornment? And there are always many who look down on what is sincere and pure and unmixed with any bitterness or gall, and who, for the sake of miserable gain, betray the care of those tropically called doves. When, therefore, the Saviour finds in the temple, the house of His Father, those who are selling oxen and sheep and doves, and the changers of money sitting, He drives them out, using the scourge of small cords which He has made, along with the sheep and oxen of their trade, and pours out their stock of coin, as not deserving to be kept together, so little is it worth. He also overturns the tables in the souls of such as love money, saying even to those who sell doves, *Take these things away* [Jn. 2, 16], that they may no longer traffic in the house of God. But I believe that in these words He indicated also a deeper truth, and that we may regard these occurrences as a symbol of the fact that the service of that temple was not any longer to be carried on by the priests in the way of material sacrifices, and that the time was coming when the law could no longer be observed, however much the Jews according to the flesh desired it. For when Jesus casts out the oxen and sheep, and orders the doves to be taken away, it was because oxen and sheep and doves were not much longer to be sacrificed there in accordance with Jewish practices. And possibly the coins which bore the stamp of material things and not of God were poured out by way of type; because the law which

69

appears so venerable, with its letter that kills, was, now that Jesus had come and had used His scourge to the people, to be dissolved and poured out, the sacred office [episcopate] being transferred to those from the Gentiles who believed, and the kingdom of God being taken away from the Jews and given to a nation bringing forth the fruits of it.

ORIGEN 58

TUESDAY OF THE FOURTH WEEK IN LENT

Moses was a type of the Savior.

While God is showing to Moses on the top of the Mountain the glorious gifts which His love is going to bestow upon His People, the latter get impatient over his absence and make a visible and therefore more "reliable" god, the molten calf. The Covenant is broken, before it has been put into effect. The sin of the People, however, is used by God to manifest His love still more gloriously. Moses shows himself in all his greatness as the true mediator between God and the People. He does not try to excuse the Israelites, but he appeals to the God of Abraham, Isaac and Jacob, to the God who has pledged everlasting love to His Chosen People. In this he succeeds. The lack of stability and faithfulness in the hearts of the Israelites causes God to disclose the "rock" of His everlasting love. The rock upon which Moses has to stand to see the "backparts" of the Lord, is a symbol of this "covenant-love" of God. The "backparts" also mean, not the unveiled Glory, but the *Mercy* which was made flesh in Christ Jesus. Standing on the rock of his faith in God's charity Moses hears the name of God proclaimed: *Jahwe, Jahwe, Elohim, merciful and gracious, patient and of much compassion and true.* [Ex. 34, 6–7] It is like a reflection of this Divine Love in Moses, the mediator, if he offers to be blotted out of the book of life rather than to see his people condemned. In this same love Christ died on the Cross for the sins of the world, and St. Paul wished himself to be accursed and cut off from Christ for the sake of his brothers, his natural kindred [Rom. 9, 3], and St. Peter, the

70

"rock" on which the Church is built laid down his life for his sheep.

Moved by Moses' entreaties God lets Mercy triumph over Justice and instead of sending an angel He Himself goes with his People. The Book of Exodus ends with the description of the Glory of God descending upon the tabernacle and filling it with the cloud of the Presence. Likewise the Passover of Christ ended with the dedication of the Church on Pentecost when the strong wind and the fiery tongues of the Spirit descended upon the Apostles. Since then the Christians are a *temple of the Lord.* [1 Cor. 3, 16] The Greek term used here by St. Paul does not mean "temple" only but—"Holy of Holies." Thus the "sign" of the tabernacle is "fulfilled": every Christian a Holy of Holies!

DAMASUS WINZEN [59]

WEDNESDAY OF THE FOURTH WEEK IN LENT

"I believe, Lord." And falling down, he worshiped him. (Gospel)

I sat on my bed and said to God, You've taken her but You haven't got me yet. I know Your cunning. It's You who take us up to a high place and offer us the whole universe. You're a devil, God, tempting us to leap. But I don't want your peace and I don't want Your love. I wanted something very simple and very easy: I wanted Sarah for a lifetime, and You took her away. With Your great schemes You ruin our happiness as a harvester ruins a mouse's nest. I hate You, God, I hate You as though You existed.

I looked at the pad of paper. It was more impersonal than a scrap of hair. You can touch hair with your lips and fingers, and I was tired to death of the mind. I had lived for her body and I wanted her body. But the journal was all I had, so I shut it back in the cupboard, for wouldn't that have been one more victory for Him, to destroy it and leave myself more completely without her? All right, have it *your* way, I said to Sarah. I believe you live and that He exists, but it will take more than your prayers to

71

turn this hatred of Him into love. He robbed me, and like that king you wrote about I'll rob Him of what He wants in me. I can't be cured like Smythe and Parkis's boy. Hatred is in my brain, not in my stomach or my skin. It can't be removed like a strawberry mark or an ache. Didn't I hate you as well as love you? And don't I hate myself?

I called down to Henry, "I'm ready," and we walked side by side over the Common towards the Pontefract Arms. The lights were out, and lovers met where the roads intersected, and on the other side of the grass was the house with the ruined steps where He gave me back this hopeless crippled life.

"I look forward to these evening walks of ours," Henry said.

"Yes."

I thought, in the morning I'll ring up a doctor and ask him whether any treatment exists. And then I thought, better not. As long as one doesn't know one can imagine innumerable cures. I put my hand on Henry's arm and held it there: I had to be strong for both of us now, and he wasn't seriously worried yet.

"They are the only things I do look forward to," Henry said.

I wrote at the start that this was a record of hate, and, walking there beside Henry towards the evening glass of beer, I found the one prayer that seemed to serve the winter mood: O God, You've done enough, You've robbed me of enough. I'm too tired and old to learn to love. Leave me alone forever.

GRAHAM GREENE [60]

We know that God spoke to Moses; but as for this man, we do not even know where he is from. (Gospel)

In the matter of God, whatever certain people may be tempted to think, it is never the proof which is lacking. What is lacking is taste for God. The most distressing diagnosis that can be made of the present age, and the most alarming, is that to all appearances at least it has lost the taste for God. Man prefers himself to God. And so he deflects the movement which leads to God; or since he is unable to alter its direction, he persists in interpreting it falsely. He imagines he has liquidated the proofs. He concentrates on the critique of the proofs and never gets beyond them. He turns away from that which convinces him. If the taste returned, we may be sure that the proofs would soon be restored in everybody's eyes, and would seem—what they really are if one considers the kernel of them—clearer than day.

HENRI DE LUBAC 61

THURSDAY OF THE FOURTH WEEK IN LENT

And he who was dead sat up and began to speak. (Gospel)

The Church has chosen the images with a sure hand. Both stories of today's Mass are of mothers in sorrow for their children, a boy and a young man. On both occasions it is God's prophet who awakens the dead child to life; for Jesus too appears in the Gospel story as the great prophet whose coming has meant God's visit to his people. In this way the *ecclesia* appears before Christ as her true prophet who brings a message of God to her and makes intercession with God on her behalf. She the widow, daily she mourns the death of her husband, the man from heaven, as she sees him dying in the mystical presence of his sacrifice on the cross. She is a widow, and doubly worthy of our pity, because her only son lies on the bier for sin, subject to its ruinous action. She is the woman whom St. John saw in the Apocalypse. *She has borne one child only, a boy, a man child* [Ap. 12, 5], the Christ child who lives and grows in each of her faithful. And this child is threatened by the dragon of sin, indeed is poisoned by it and lies dead before her. She weeps for this child, for the dead Christ, the dead life in her faithful. She begs on its behalf before the great prophet, the man of God. Her faith is boundless, for she knows that he is the prophet and the man of God. The one of whom all the others were only types, in whose power they all did what they did. And she knows that this unique one is her heavenly spouse, that he who dies daily lives for ever; that, although a widow, she is still a bride, and that her husband awakens daily himself and her child as well, the divine life she has received of him and born in her faithful. Her children have been awakened from the death of sin, and brought by

73

Christ, her spouse, out of the grave. Because she knows all of this, even in the midst of her trouble and her sorrow she has comfort and the certainty that she will be raised once more.

AEMILIANA LOHR [62]

FRIDAY OF THE FOURTH WEEK IN LENT

I am the resurrection and the life. (Gospel)

But most surprising is the peculiar freedom we find in Jesus' attitude towards death. Not the freedom of the hero who considers death's victory the simple reversal of greatness; also not the freedom of the sage, who has perceived what is lost in death and what remains, and firmly stands his ground. Here is something else. Essentially Jesus knows himself independent of death because death has no claim on him. No part of him is "stung" by mortality; perfect fruit, he is sound to the core.

Because he is entirely alive Jesus dominates death. Death's superior, he voluntarily submits to it, he who has been sent into the world to change death's very essence in the eyes of God.

The freedom Jesus takes with death is most obvious in the raising of the three dead. We see it when he restores the son to the widow of Naim, effortlessly calling the youth back to live as he passes through the city gates. [Lk. 7, 11–17] And when the Lord returns his little daughter to Jairus with such delicate, lovely ease—*the girl is asleep, not dead* [Mk. 5, 40]—he seems to be playing with death. The terrible one obeys his almost bantering word, and withdraws as lightly as slumber from a child's lids at the waking hand of a mother. Finally, the tremendous event that John describes in his eleventh chapter: the resurrection of Lazarus . . .

I am the resurrection and the life; he who believes in me, even if he die, shall live. . . . The words span heaven and earth: *I am the resurrection and the life,* I and no other. Everything depends on our accomplishing within ourselves this "I am." If only Jesus' vitality were in us, we should not know death. But that vital quality which in Jesus is not only indestructible, but

74

intrinsic and creative, has been destroyed in us. Hence we die. Our death is not "tacked on" to life, it is the direct outcome of the kind of life we live. In our dying a condition already present in our living asserts itself: a condition—as we see by contrast with Jesus, the full measure of man—which should not exist. Mortality has no foothold in Jesus. For this reason, although he offered himself up in the Eucharist and died the death on the cross, he exists only as "life": (for us, who are mortal, as "the Resurrection"). Thus the human being linked in faith to Christ possesses a life that will outlive death and that already here on earth reaches into eternity. It is as Christ himself once expressed it: *Amen, amen, I say to you, he who hears my word, and believes him who sent me, has life everlasting, and does not come to judgment, but has passed from death to life.* [Jn. 5, 24].

ROMANO GUARDINI [63]

Life has taught me that in this world nobody is consoled who has not first consoled another and that we get back only what we have first given away. Among us men there are only exchanges; God alone gives, He alone.

GEORGES BERNANOS [64]

SATURDAY OF THE FOURTH WEEK IN LENT

I am the light of the world. (Gospel)

He who follows Me, says Christ our Saviour, *walks not in darkness, for he will have the light of life.* These are the words of our Lord Jesus Christ, and by them we are admonished to follow His teachings and His manner of living, if we would truly be enlightened and delivered from all blindness of heart.

Let all the study of our heart be from now on to have our meditation fixed wholly on the life of Christ, for His holy teachings are of more virtue and strength than the words of all the angels and saints. And he who through grace has the inner eye of his soul opened to the true beholding of the Gospels of Christ will find in them hidden manna.

75

It is often seen that those who hear the Gospels find little sweetness in them; the reason is that they do not have the spirit of Christ. So, if we desire to have a true understanding of His Gospels, we must study to conform our life as nearly as we can to His.

What avail is it to a man to reason about the high, secret mysteries of the Trinity if he lack humility and so displeases the Holy Trinity? Truly, it avails nothing. Deeply inquisitive reasoning does not make a man holy or righteous, but a good life makes him beloved by God. I would rather feel compunction of heart for my sins than merely know the definition of compunction. If you know all the books of the Bible merely by rote and all the sayings of the philosophers by heart, what will it profit you without grace and charity? All that is in the world is vanity except to love God and to serve Him only. This is the most noble and the most excellent wisdom that can be in any creature: by despising the world to draw daily nearer and nearer to the kingdom of heaven.

It is therefore a great vanity to labor inordinately for worldly riches that will shortly perish or to covet honor or any other inordinate pleasures or fleshly delights in this life, for which a man after this life will be sorely and grievously punished. How great a vanity it also is to desire a long life and to care little for a good life; to heed things of the present and not to provide for things that are to come; to love things that will shortly pass away and not to haste to where joy is everlasting. Have this common proverb often in your mind: The eye is not satisfied or pleased with seeing any material thing, nor the ear with hearing. Study, therefore, to withdraw the love of your soul from all things that are visible, and to turn it to things that are invisible. Those who follow their own sensuality hurt their own cause and lose the grace of God.

THOMAS A KEMPIS [65]

Passion Time

FIRST SUNDAY OF THE PASSION

As the celebration of the paschal mystery draws near our eyes turn more and more toward the Cross and all it signifies of both death and life.

Christ has appeared, High Priest of the good things to come.
(Epistle)

God is love. In order to raise us to His divine life, He created the world with man its king. Since man is an intelligent being and created in God's image, he is destined on behalf of himself and of all creatures to be the adorer of the infinite Being. But Adam accepted no other sovereign but himself; that is his sin. Relations are severed. The original order is destroyed. Who shall re-establish ties with the Creator? Man is incapable of doing so. But God "Who in a wonderful manner didst create everything, in His mercy wants to renew it still more wonderfully." He decides to send His Son to men, as Pontiff, *Pontifex,* which can be translated as "the builder of bridges." He shall be their ferry, as it were, the passageway between God and men. Christ Himself acknowledges this explicitly: *Ego sum via, I am the Way.* [Jn. 14, 6] He is the only way, that is to say, the unique Mediator between creation and its Creator, and hence the sole Priest.

This teaching has been magnificently supported by the whole of patristic and theological tradition. Both demonstrate that Christ's priesthood follows directly from His Incarnation, that is to say, as a result of the hypostatic union.

St. Augustine puts it formally: "In that He is born of the Father, God of God, He is not a priest. He is Priest because of the flesh which He assumed, because of the victim He received from us for the purpose of offering it.

"Indeed, the Son of God is only a priest according to His human nature, for priesthood involves a real submission to God. However, human nature possesses in Him the sacerdotal dignity only because it subsists in the person of the Word, so that His priesthood holds its existence, its dignity, its power and its superiority from the hypostatic union. It belongs, in fact, to the human nature of Christ, as a sacerdotal consecration conferred upon Him at the very instant of the Incarnation in the womb of the Blessed Virgin Mary; and the indissolubility of the hypostatic union is the basis of the everlasting priesthood of Christ." Although it will never end, Christ's priesthood had however a beginning in time. The Word, only Son of God, was not a priest before coming to us: "It was at the moment of His Incarnation that the Word made flesh became Priest: As long as he remains in the bosom of His Father He can neither abase Himself, worship, nor pray." . . .

There are not several priesthoods, there is only one, that of Christ: "Others have had some participation of the priesthood: He has it in its entirety, or rather, He does not so much have it as be it. He is all the priesthood . . . Besides He is not a priest among priests, greater than the others or holier. He is the unique Priest . . . He exhausts in Himself . . . all priesthood."

There are not, therefore, several kinds or degrees of priests, as if each one were a separate kind of priest. *The priesthood cannot be invented, it is.* It is not even, in a sense, something. It is someone: Christ.

Christ, Priest; two interchangeable titles. *Ipso facto* that priesthood is complete and perfect; no one can add anything to it.

It is a permanent mediation, wrought upon earth on the Cross and consummated in Heaven where Christ *lives on still to make intercession on our behalf.* [Heb. 7, 25]

EMMANUEL SUHARD [66]

The Tree of Knowledge and the Cross.

The sin that was wrought through the tree was undone by the obedience of the tree, obedience to God whereby the Son of man was nailed to the tree, destroying the knowledge of evil, and bringing in and conferring the knowledge of good; and evil is disobedience to God, as obedience to God is good. And therefore the Word says through Isaias the prophet, foretelling what was to come to pass in the future—for it was because they told the future that they were "prophets"—the Word says through him as follows: *I refuse not, and do not gainsay, my back have I delivered to blows and my cheeks to buffets, and I have not turned away my face from the contumely of them that spat.* [Is. 50, 6] So by obedience, whereby He obeyed unto death, hanging on the tree, He undid the old disobedience wrought in the tree. And because He is Himself the Word of God Almighty, who in His invisible form pervades us universally in the whole world, and encompasses both its length and breadth and height and depth—for by God's Word everything is disposed and administered—the Son of God was also crucified in these, imprinted in the form of a cross on the universe; for He had necessarily, in becoming visible, to bring to light the universality of His cross, in order to show openly through His visible form that activity of His: that it is He who makes bright the height, that is, what is in heaven, and holds the deep, which is in the bowels of the earth, and stretches forth and extends the length from East to West, navigating also the Northern parts and the breadth of the South, and calling in all the dispersed from all sides to the knowledge of the Father.

ST. IRENAEUS [67]

MONDAY IN PASSION TIME

Rivers of living water. (Gospel)

Let our heart only be athirst, and be ready to receive: in the
degree in which we bring to it a capacious faith, in that measure
we draw from it an overflowing grace.

ST. CYPRIAN OF CARTHAGE [68]

By saying: *As the Scripture says, from within him shall flow
rivers of living water* [Jn. 7, 38], He is alluding to the wealth
and abundance of grace. He spoke in a similar vein elsewhere:
A fountain of water, springing up unto life everlasting, that is,
he who drinks of the water that I will give him, will have much
grace. [Jn. 4, 14]

In another context, then, He said "life everlasting," while here
He speaks of "living water." And by "living" He means "ever-
active." For, when the grace of the Spirit enters into the soul
and takes up its abode there, it gushes forth more abundantly
than any fountain and does not cease, nor become exhausted, nor
stand still. Well, then, to show at the same time its unceasing attendance upon the soul and its ineffable activity He called it "a
fountain" and "rivers": not one river, but rivers without number.
And in the other context He indicated its generous flow by the
word "springing up."

Moreover, one may see clearly what is meant if one considers
the wisdom of Stephen, the fluency of Peter, and the forceful-
ness of Paul, and notices how nothing could oppose them, nothing withstand them: whether popular fury, or violence of tyrants,
or plots of demons, or daily deaths—but, like rivers borne along
with rushing turbulence, they swept all aside and carried it off.
He said this of the Spirit, the Evangelist said, *whom they who
believed in him were to receive; for the Holy Spirit was not yet
with them.* [Jn. 7, 39–40]

ST. JOHN CHRYSOSTOM [69]

Arm yourselves with . . . the sword of the spirit which is the word of God. (Epistle)

One text in St. John shows us that the opened side of Christ in glory is the source whence the books of the New Testament flow:

> *If any man thirst, let him come to me, and let him that believeth in me drink. As the Scripture saith: Out of his belly shall flow rivers of living water.*

From Christ's belly the rivers will flow—we should translate this Hebrew phrase by saying they will flow from Christ's heart. And *this he said of the Spirit which they should receive who believed in him;* he said it of the Holy Spirit whose tremendous outpouring in the last days had been spoken of by the Prophets. From Christ's sacred body where the soldier's lance struck him, as from the rock of Sinai, would flow the rivers of the New Testament, all the graces of the Kingdom, and also those of Scripture—the graces by which Scripture would be inspired, by which it would be read and understood, by which it would give life to the world. All these rivers will flow from that open side on the day of his redeeming glory. Until that day, *the Spirit was not given, because Jesus was not yet glorified.* [Jn. 7, 27–29] "O heart of my beloved," cried St. John Eudes, "I adore you as the source of all the holy words in this book." The Evangelists came, and each drank from that spring. "He drank the rivers of the gospel from the sacred fount of the Lord's heart," we say of the Apostle John in the office for his feast.

The New Testament is not Christ's book because it tells his story; it is his book because it is from him, born out of the wound in his heart, born like a child. Every word of Scripture is a grace of the Spirit of Jesus, a thought of everlasting life which flowed from his heart along with his blood: *And there came out blood and water,* [Jn. 19, 34] the water of the Spirit with the blood of immolation. With their sure instincts, the saints felt this redeeming presence in the New Testament. St. Ignatius of Antioch wrote: "I take refuge in the Gospel as in the flesh of Jesus Christ."

81

Other saints were to love to hide in Christ's heart, but St. Ignatius sought his refuge in the Gospel, in the revelation of the Christian mystery, for that gospel was like a sacrament of the redeeming Christ, like a field in which, as St. Jerome said, the treasure was hidden, the treasure of Christ himself.

F. X. DURRWELL [70]

TUESDAY IN PASSION TIME

Some said: "He is a good man"; others said: "No, he is leading the people astray." (Gospel)

When we meet a saint we are not discovering at long last an ideal, lived and realised, which had already been formed within us. A saint is not the perfection of humanity—or of the super-man—incarnate in a particular man. The marvel is of a different order. What we find is a new life, a new sphere of existence, with unsuspected depths—but also with a resonance hitherto unknown to us and now at last revealed. We are shown a new country, a home we had originally ignored, and as soon as we perceive it we recognise it as older and truer than anything we had known and with claims upon our heart.

No feeling of self-satisfaction invades us; we do not see our noblest image reflected in a mirror. This is not the fulfilment of our loveliest dream—or rather there is something further, which is not only more beautiful: we are simultaneously attracted and repelled, and the more we are repelled the more we are attracted. We experience an ambiguous sensation as of something at the same time very near and very far; something disturbing, troubling and at the same time obscurely desired. The feeling is a mixed one, compounded of a sense of strangeness and of supreme fulfilment beyond all desire. We are both disconcerted and ravished, and the delight we experience is never without a sense of dread. Our worldliness reacts to the threat. Our secret connivance with evil is aroused. We are on our guard. If we had begun to regard ourselves as perfect in some respect, we shall be doubly tempted to reject the provoking vista which is going to oblige us to recognise our misery and, more than that, the wretchedness of what we call perfection.

But in all this we are not left to ourselves, as spectators. It acts upon us as a provocation. It is a summons to choose and to act, unveiling our most hidden tendencies. . . . All of a sudden the universe seems different; it is the stage of a vast drama, and we, at its heart, are compelled to play our part.

If there were more saints in the world, the spiritual struggle would only be more intense. As the Kingdom of God becomes more manifest, it calls forth more fervent adherents—and, correspondingly, more violent opposition. The heightened urgency of the situation provokes tension and becomes the occasion of resounding conflicts.

For if we are more or less at peace in the world, it is simply that we are tepid.

HENRI DE LUBAC [71]

WEDNESDAY IN PASSION TIME

I and the Father are one. (Gospel)

At these words thought fails and our tongue stumbles. The conception they express is staggering. Once upon a time, within historical memory, there lived a man, thoroughly sound in mind and body, who was gifted with an unusually lucid insight into the facts of existence, into the greatest as well as the least, and with extraordinarily keen understanding. He was a man who was more selfless and unself-seeking than anyone who has ever lived, and whose life was devoted to the service of the poor and the oppressed. And this healthy, clear-sighted, selfless man, from beginning to end of his life, knew himself to be the unique well-beloved Son of the Father, to be one who knew the Father as no other man could. More than this, there was once a man, within historical times, who, as a child of the Jewish people, knew only of one God of heaven and earth, of a unique Father in heaven, and stood in reverential awe before this heavenly Father: a man whose meat was to do the will of this Father, who from his ear-

83

liest youth in good days and bad had sought and loved this will alone, whose whole life was one prayer; a man, further, whose whole being was so firmly united with this Divine will, that by its omnipotence he healed the sick and restored the dead to life; a man, finally, who was so intimately and exclusively dedicated to this will, that he never swerved from it, so that not even the slightest consciousness of sin ever oppressed him, so that never a cry of penance and forgiveness passed his lips, so that even in dying he begged pardon not for himself but for others. And this man from the intimacy of his union with God could say to afflicted mortals, *Thy sins are forgiven thee?* [Mt. 9, 2] And it was this holy man, utterly subject as he was to God throughout his whole life, absorbed as he was in God, awestruck as he stood before him, who asserted, as if it were the most natural and obvious thing in the world, that he was to be the judge of the world at the last day, that he was the suffering servant of God, nay more, that he was the only begotten Son of God and consubstantial with him, and could say of himself, *I and the Father are one.*

Can we, may we, dare we give credence to this man? We are asked to believe in the Incarnation of God, that is to say, we are asked to accept the fact that God so humbled himself as to *empty* himself, to use St. Paul's words, of his Divine majesty. [Phil. 2, 7] Is it not our duty to conclude that a man was mistaken, though he were the holiest who ever lived, rather than to believe that God would humble himself so immeasurably? Is not a man here rising up against God? Is it not in the last resort unbelief, if we believe? Does not our alert, reverential sense of God's uniqueness and eternal majesty actually oblige us to refuse our assent and either, like Caiaphas, to rend our garments and to cry out: *He hath blasphemed,* or with his kindred to lament his madness? Must we not, with Chesterton, rather "expect the grass to wither and the birds to drop dead out of the air, when a strolling carpenter's apprentice says calmly and almost carelessly, like one looking over his shoulder: *Before Abraham was I am, I and the Father are one.*

We can only say that a man who at this point, when confronted with the paradox of God the all-perfect, all-holy, eternal, becoming a man, a carpenter, a Jew haled before the court and crucified, shrinks away, can go no further, and breaks down, may be actually less remote from a living piety than one who coolly accepts all this and glibly repeats his Credo, or indeed than one who does homage to the noble humanity of Jesus yet has the temerity to pooh-pooh what Jesus said of himself as harmless rhetoric, the innocent exaggerations of a pious eccentric.

KARL ADAM [72]

THURSDAY IN PASSION TIME

Many sins are forgiven her because she has loved much. (Gospel)

The Pharisee asked Christ to eat. What did the woman who was not asked seek there? A stranger does not burst into the interior of a house. An uninvited man does not dare to enter its private banquet room. A reckless spectator does not dare to disturb the foods made ready to relax spirits weary after labor. Why, then, does this woman, unknown—or rather of bad reputation—burdened with grief, weeping copiously, lamenting aloud, with the doorkeeper unaware, and everyone else, too, even the Shepherd Himself—why does she run through all the doors, pass through all the groups of servants, fly even to the private hall of the banquet, and turn the whole house of joy into one of lamentation and wailing?

Brethren, she did not come uninvited; she was under command. She entered not as one rashly daring, but as one ushered in. He who ordered her to be absolved by a heavenly judgment is the One who caused her to be brought to Himself. The well-dressed Pharisee was reclining at the first place on his banquet couch, swelling with pride before the very eyes of Christ. In order to please men, not God, he was gaily engrossed in his banquet. At that time the woman came. She came up from behind, because a guilty soul seeking pardon stands behind the pardoner's back. She knew that because of her guilt she had lost the confidence to stand before His face.

When she came, she came to make satisfaction to God, not to please men. She came to provide a banquet of devotion, not of pleasure. She set a table of repentance, served courses of compunction and the bread of sorrow. She mixed the drink with tears in proper measure, and to the full delight of God she struck music from her heart and body. She produced the organ tones of her lamentations, played upon the zither by her long and rhythmical sighs, and fitted her groans to the flute. While she kept striking her breast in reproach to her conscience she made the cymbals resound which would please God. While she set foods like these before God's sight, she received abundant mercy.

ST. PETER CHRYSOLOGUS [73]

FRIDAY IN PASSION TIME

Jesus was to die . . . to gather into unity the scattered children of God. (Gospel)

Christ our Passover lamb has been sacrificed, writes St. Paul. [1 Cor. 5, 7] The apostle saw that the Passover contained, in figure and symbol, the mystery of Christ; for the sacrifice of Jesus is the real Passover by which the true Israel, the Church, is delivered from the hard bonds of Satan and sin, is protected on her journey to the Promised Land, and is finally admitted to the peace of perfect union with God in heaven. As the Israelites in Egypt were saved by the blood of the Passover lamb sprinkled on their doorposts, so we are redeemed by Christ's precious blood, as of a lamb unblemished in God's sight. By the shedding of his blood, Christ instituted the undying paschal mystery. Christ's death is the true sacrifice, and in it all earlier worship is consummated.

Truly do we glory in the cross of our Lord Jesus Christ, for in him is our salvation, our life and resurrection; through him we have been saved and made free. With him there is copious redemption. Good Friday's story is not one of gloom and doom; it is one of joy, it is the story of delivery. Like a new Moses Christ leads his people out of the dark land of slavery into the light of

86

the kingdom of God. Like Moses raising the brazen serpent in the wilderness, Christ lifts high the cross on which he himself was lifted up. It is the sign of salvation; it is the sign of victory.

And therefore on Good Friday, while we contemplate the salvific paradox of the cross, the Church causes us to realize what could not be discovered by those who crucified the Lord of glory —that in the cross is our glorification. Our concern with the death of Christ, accepted in all its stark realism, blends through faith and love with our acknowledgment of the divine glory that is included in that death, and of our redemption accomplished by it. Once we were darkness; now, in the Lord, we are all daylight. For the light of Christ leads us, like a pillar of fire, through the desert of this world into the celestial Land of Promise.

FRANCIS A. BRUNNER [74]

SATURDAY IN PASSION TIME

And I, if I be lifted up from the earth, shall draw all things to myself. (Gospel)

That which was done against our Lord Jesus Christ by false witnesses, by cruel rulers, by impious priests, using the ministry of a cowardly governor, and the attendance of an ignorant cohort, has been in all ages a matter to be at once detested and embraced. For as the Cross of our Lord, in regard to the mind of the Jews, was cruel, so in regard to the power of the Crucified it is marvellous. The people rages against One, and Christ has mercy on all. What is inflicted by ferocity is welcomed by free will, so that the audacity of the crime accomplishes the work of the eternal Will. Wherefore the whole order of events, which the Gospel narrative goes through so fully, is in such a manner to be received by the ears of the faithful, that while we entirely believe in the acts which were performed at the time of our Lord's Passion, we are to understand that in Christ was not only remission of sins accomplished, but also a pattern of righteousness displayed.

ST. LEO THE GREAT [75]

HOLY WEEK

Instead of being a commentary on the day's liturgy, the following texts are designed to open the reader's mind and heart to the sufferings of Jesus and all their blessed consequences. Each day the Church presents and considers the Paschal Mystery as a whole, but each day also from a different point of view.

Oh, Loving Madman! was it not enough for Thee to become Incarnate, that Thou must also die?

ST. CATHERINE OF SIENA [76]

The wonderful works of God among the people of the Old Testament were but a prelude to the work of Christ the Lord in redeeming mankind and giving perfect glory to God. He achieved his task principally by the paschal mystery of his blessed passion, resurrection from the dead, and glorious ascension, whereby *dying, he destroyed our death and, rising, he restored our life.* For it was from the side of Christ as he slept the sleep of death upon the cross that there came forth *the wondrous sacrament of the whole Church.*

CONSTITUTION ON THE SACRED LITURGY [77]

Let us hasten, O believers, moving from one divine festival to another; from palms and branches to the fulfillment of the august and saving sufferings of Christ. Let us watch him, bearing his sufferings voluntarily for our sake; and let us sing unto him with worthy praise, crying, O Fountain of mercy, O Haven of salvation, O Lord, glory to you. . . .

Because of a tree, Adam was estranged from paradise; and the thief because of the tree of the Cross abode in paradise; for the former in tasting, disobeyed the commandment of the Creator; but the latter, who was crucified with you, confessed, admitting to you that you are a hidden God. Wherefore, O Saviour, remember him and us in your kingdom. . . .

Your life-bearing side, O Christ, overflows like a spring from

88

Eden, watering your Church as a paradise endowed with speech; and thence divides the glad tidings into four Gospels, as into four heads, watering the world, gladdening creation, and teaching the Gentiles to adore your kingdom in faith. . . .

You were crucified, O Christ, for my sake, that you might pour forth salvation for me. And your side was pierced with a spear, that it might cause rivers of life to flow for me. You were fastened with the nails; and so realizing the depth of your Passion and the height of your might, I will cry unto you, Glory to your Passion and to your Crucifixion, O life-giving Saviour.

BYZANTINE LITURGY [78]

The Mystery of Jesus.

Jesus suffers in His passions the torments which men inflict upon Him; but in His agony He suffers the torments which He inflicts upon Himself. This is a suffering from no human, but an almighty hand, for He must be almighty to bear it.

Jesus seeks some comfort at least in His three dearest friends, and they are asleep. He prays them to bear with Him for a little, and they leave Him with entire indifference, having so little compassion that it could not prevent their sleeping even for a moment. And thus Jesus was left alone to the wrath of God.

Jesus is alone on the earth, without anyone not only to feel and share His suffering, but even to know of it; He and Heaven were alone in that knowledge.

Jesus is in a garden, not of delight as the first Adam, where he lost himself and the whole human race, but in one of agony, where He saved Himself and the whole human race.

He suffers this affliction and this desertion in the horror of night.

I believe that Jesus never complained but on this single occasion; but then He complained as if he could no longer bear His extreme suffering. *My soul is sorrowful, even unto death.* [Mt. 26, 38]

Jesus seeks companionship and comfort from men. This is the sole occasion in all His life, as it seems to me. But He receives it not, for His disciples are asleep.

89

Jesus will be in agony even to the end of the world. We must not sleep during that time.

Jesus, in the midst of this universal desertion, including that of His own friends chosen to watch with Him, finding them asleep, is vexed because of the danger to which they expose, not Him, but themselves; He cautions them for their own safety and their own good, with a sincere tenderness for them during their ingratitude, and warns them that the spirit is willing and the flesh weak.

Jesus, finding them still asleep, without being restrained by any consideration for themselves or for Him, has the kindness not to waken them, and leaves them in repose.

Jesus prays, uncertain of the will of His Father, and fears death; but, when He knows it, He goes forward to offer Himself to death.

Jesus, asked of men and was not heard.

Jesus, while His disciples slept, wrought their salvation. He has wrought that of each of the righteous while they slept, both in their nothingness before their birth, and in their sins after their birth.

He prays only once that the cup pass away, and then with submission; and twice that it come if necessary.

Jesus is weary.

Jesus, seeing all His friends asleep and all His enemies wakeful, commits Himself entirely to His Father.

Jesus does not regard in Judas his enmity, but the order of God, which He loves and admits, since He calls him friend.

Jesus tears Himself away from His disciples to enter into His agony; we must tear ourselves away from our nearest and dearest to imitate Him.

Jesus being in agony and in the greatest affliction, let us pray longer.

We implore the mercy of God, not that He may leave us at peace in our vices, but that He may deliver us from them.

If God gave us masters by His own hand, Oh! how necessary for us to obey them with a good heart! Necessity and events follow infallibly.

—"Console thyself, thou wouldst not seek Me, if thou hadst not found Me.

"I thought of thee in Mine agony, I have sweated such drops of blood for thee.

"It is tempting Me rather than proving thyself, to think if thou wouldst do such and such a thing on an occasion which has not happened; I shall act in thee if it occur.

"Let thyself be guided by My rules; see how well I have led the Virgin and the saints who have let Me act in them.

"The Father loves all that I do.

"Dost thou wish that it always cost Me the blood of My humanity, without thy shedding tears?

"Thy conversion is My affair; fear not, and pray with confidence as for Me. . . .

"I am present with thee by My Word in scripture, by My Spirit in the Church and by inspiration, by My power in the priests, by My prayer in the faithful.

"Physicians will not heal thee, for thou wilt die at last. But it is I who heal thee, and make the body immortal.

"Suffer bodily chains and servitude, I deliver thee at present only from spiritual servitude.

"I am more a friend to thee than such and such an one, for I have done for thee more than they; they would not have suffered what I have suffered from thee, and they would not have died for thee as I have done in the time of thine infidelities and cruelties, and as I am ready to do, and do, among My elect and at the Holy Sacrament."

"If thou knewest thy sins, thou wouldst lose heart."

—I shall lose it then, Lord, for on Thy assurance I believe their malice.

—"No, for I, by whom thou learnest, can heal thee of them, and what I say to thee is a sign that I will heal thee. In proportion to thy expiation of them, thou wilt know them, and it will be said to thee: 'Behold, thy sins are forgiven thee.' Repent, then, for thy hidden sins, and for the secret malice of those which thou knowest."

—Lord, I give Thee all.

BLAISE PASCAL [79]

91

"Rabbi," he said; and kissed him.

There is hardly one of us who has not known what it is to be betrayed. We used to find the figure of Judas an enigma, but now we know him only too well. The air we breathe is so infested with mistrust that it almost chokes us. But where we have managed to pierce through this layer of mistrust we have discovered a confidence scarce dreamed of hitherto. Where we do trust we have learnt to entrust our very lives to the hands of others. In face of all the many constructions to which our actions and our lives have been inevitably exposed we have learnt to trust without reserve. We know that hardly anything can be more reprehensible than the sowing and encouragement of mistrust, and that our duty is rather to do everything in our power to strengthen and foster confidence among men. Trust will always be one of the greatest, rarest and happiest blessings of social life, though it can only emerge on the dark background of a necessary mistrust. We have learnt never to trust a scoundrel an inch, but to give ourselves to the trustworthy without reserve.

DIETRICH BONHOEFFER [80]

The Cosmic Tree.

This wood of the cross is mine for my eternal salvation. I am nourished by it, I feast on it. I am strengthened in its roots, I lie down under its branches, I fill my nostrils with its savor as with a sweet breeze. This tree, which stretches up to the sky, goes from earth to heaven. Immortal plant, it stands midway between heaven and earth, a strong prop for the universe, binding all things together, supporting the whole inhabited earth, a cosmic interlacing which embraces the whole motley of humanity; the Spirit holds it firm with invisible nails so that its contact with God may never be loosened, as it touches heaven with its peak, keeps its base firmly on the earth, and embraces all the atmosphere between with its measureless arms.

He was completely everywhere, in all things, yet there, alone and bare, He struggled against immaterial forces. When His cosmic battle came to an end, the heavens shook, the stars were near to falling, the sun was darkened for a time, stones were split open, and the world might well have perished, but Christ gave up His soul, saying: *Father, into thy hands I commend my spirit.* [Lk. 23, 46] And then, when He ascended, His divine spirit gave life and strength to the tottering world, and the whole universe became stable once more, as if the stretching out, the agony of the Cross, had in some way got into everything. Thou who art all in all, may thy spirit be in heaven, and thy soul in paradise, but may thy blood be on the earth.

ST. HIPPOLYTUS OF ROME [81]

What died in Mary's heart on the eve of Christ's Passion was the merely human love she still had for Christ as her human son: what was born in her heart on the day He rose was her universal motherhood of all men. For this to happen, it is quite true to say that something in her heart had to die: it was the end of a great happiness, of the thirty-three years she had lived with God made man. That is why, when Christ, indicating John, said to her, *Woman, behold thy son* [Jn. 19, 26], a sword pierced deep into her heart, it was the end of a marvelous reality. At that moment she went beyond the love concentrated on the humanity of Jesus, she opened her heart wide enough to include the whole of humanity. This could only be done by death, by that death of the heart, by as deep a suffering in her heart as our Lord had in His Body; for this, too, this growth of charity, this outgoing of love that was to embrace the world, could only come about through death.

JEAN DANIELOU [82]

THE THREE DAYS OF THE PASCHAL MYSTERY

To say that the Easter observances are the center of the ecclesiastical year leaves much untold: they are the center where all the liturgy converges and the spring whence it all flows. All Christian worship is but a continuous celebration of Easter: the sun, rising and setting daily, leaves in its wake an uninterrupted series of Eucharists; every Mass that is celebrated prolongs the pasch. Each day of the liturgical year and, within each day, every instant of the sleepless life of the Church, continues and renews the pasch that Our Lord had desired with such great desire to eat with His disciples while awaiting the pasch He should eat in His kingdom, the pasch to be prolonged for all eternity. The annual pasch, which we are constantly recalling or anticipating, preserves us ever in the sentiment of the early Christians, who exclaimed, looking to the past, "The Lord is risen indeed," and turning towards the future, *Come, Lord Jesus! Come! Make no delay.* [Ap. 22, 20]

LOUIS BOUYER [83]

The mystery of the paschal triduum, or last three days of Holy Week, which begins with Holy Thursday and closes with the night of the Resurrection, is only the mystery of every daily Mass. But the Mass of Holy Thursday is the Mass par excellence, brought close to its source. In the primitive plenitude of its rites and of their significance, it sums up in itself that vast accumulation of blessings which scatter its graces upon the whole life of man and of the world. Like the Last Supper, it combines solemnity and hope, in the heartbreaking thought of Good Friday and the glorious visions of the paschal night. The liturgy of the other two days is only the expansion of the Holy Thursday Mass, reaffirming its historic significance in our Leader's cross, and its eschatological meaning in the glory of the Mystical Body. This meaning implied in every Mass is unfolded in the liturgy of these three days with the maximum not only of exactness but also of poetry. Their successive events constitute only a full and impressive eucharistic celebration with two motifs, where all the phases of the Mass appear in order. At the Mass of Holy Thursday, we see the Last Supper as forerunner of the cross. At the Mass of Holy Saturday, the cross, its work accomplished, will reproduce the Last Supper, but this time in the fadeless light of the Resurrection.

LOUIS BOUYER [84]

HOLY THURSDAY

On this day the Lord instituted the Eucharist, sharing the meal that through ages should unite His members in and through Himself.

Today is therefore the day of Christian community, and of divine and fraternal charity.

Because a wooden table is anciently venerated as that of the Last Supper in the cathedral church of St. John Lateran in Rome, the seat of our chief bishop Paul, the Vicar of Christ, leads his Roman flock there in the banquet of charity and unity.

This evening we are gathered in spirit—in the Spirit—with the apostles to receive from Jesus the gift of His flesh and blood, as it were, for the first time.

The altar breads will be freshly consecrated, and afterwards the ordinary bread of mealtime will be blessed and eaten at table. The reason for the twofold celebration, each one sacred though in a different sense, is that

The love of Christ has brought us together.

Let us love the living God and love each other with single hearts.

This is the Thursday of the Lord's Supper. We think of ourselves, even feel ourselves, to be like disciples in the upper room gathered about the Master for a fraternal meal.

This is a Mass of Christian unity in a special way, for Jesus gave His friends a moving discourse about their unity on this night.

He prayed, *Father, keep them true to my name, that they may be one, as we are one.* [Jn. 17, 12]

In every church and chapel throughout Christendom, all the faithful are gathered in unity to partake of the one sacred banquet.

This morning in the cathedral churches of the world there was offered the Mass of the Chrism, that celebration in which the oil of rich olives is mixed with aromatic balm and blessed by a bishop for sacred use.

We would be incapable of Christian worship, you may say, were it not for the activity in our cathedral in this city this morning. How can the brow and crown of the newly baptized be anointed without the oil of gladness? How can the souls of the baptized be sealed or imprinted in the Spirit except by the chrism with which their foreheads are signed with Christ's cross? How can there be a sacrificial offering of the Lord's Supper except a priesthood has had its hands anointed with chrism, once a bishop has first laid on his own? How can the senses be healed with the anointing of the sick if there is no ointment?

The events of Holy Thursday morning are a sacramental prerequisite for the events of this evening.

Christ writhed in spirit in an olive grove. In the midst of these gnarled trees, with an olive-press close by, He grew sorrowful even unto death. But He in His turn enriched us by the olive. He made it the sign of spiritual power in His kingdom. A sign of prosperity and wealth it had always been; the sign of sacral kingship and priesthood and the prophet's office, ancient Israel later made it. Jesus made olive oil to be the sign of a sharing in His priesthood—He who is our first anointed priest, our Christos.

And so when we are reborn in water and the Spirit, oil reminds us that a share in Christ's saving work has been given us. We can join in offering the fitting sacrifice, now that we are confirmed, that is, have the fullness of the Spirit. From among the royal priesthood and holy people of the baptized some are set apart for priestly ordination, and oil is the sign of it once more.

There is no Eucharist, in other words, apart from chrism.

There is no banquet of charity, with shoots of the young olive gathered round the Father's table, unless the olive tree has first yielded its fruit.

This evening's Mass is a blend of joy and sadness. There is joy because the Church celebrates the great gift of the body of Christ. There is sadness, for we cannot fail to recall it was a farewell meal Jesus was taking with His disciples. There was cast over it, moreover, the terrible treachery of a friend.

It is by receiving the Eucharist that we most clearly share in the sacrificial action—priest and people eating together the Victim they have offered together.

We take this meal then, in a spirit of love, a spirit of unity, a spirit of faith, a spirit of fidelity.

May we be separated, cut off, from no one—least of all from

Christ or from each other—we who eat the one loaf which makes us one, even as Jesus and His Father are one.

GERARD S. SLOYAN [85]

The Radiant Cross.

That is the explanation of the paradoxical fact that the cross in the paschal liturgy appears as a symbol, not of Christ's defeat, but of His victory. *Nos autem oportet gloriari in cruce Domini nostri Jesu Christi,* proclaims the Introit of the Mass of Holy Thursday, introducing the leitmotiv that will recur all this day and the following: *We must glory in the cross of our Lord Jesus Christ.* [Gal. 6, 14] That is, moreover, exactly what Jesus declared in the first words of His sacerdotal prayer (so called because He refers there to His voluntary sacrifice): *Father, the hour is come, glorify thy Son that thy Son may glorify thee.* [Jn. 17, 1] This glorification of Christ, here as everywhere else in the fourth Gospel (which constantly uses the expression), is the cross.

All devotion to the cross known to Christian antiquity, particularly under the influence of the Jerusalem liturgy after the pilgrimages to the Holy Land, is only a hymn of victory. Fortunatus, singing of the approach of the Passion, begins with these words: *Vexilla Regis prodeunt, fulget crucis mysterium* (The standards of the King advance, the mystery of the cross shines resplendent). The first Christians were so far from separating the cross from the Resurrection that they represented Christ in glory even on the crucifix. The Resurrection was for them not a reparation for, but the fruit of, the cross.

This is believable only if we do not separate Good Friday from Holy Thursday. On Good Friday the executioners are active; Jesus does naught but suffer. Holy Thursday, because it is the hour of the eucharistic banquet, provides background for the treason of Judas and the consequences of his act because it shows us Christ delivering Himself as a sacrifice for men: *Take and eat, this is my body given for you. . . . drink, this is the chalice of the New Testament in my blood shed in remission for sins for you and for many.* That is clearly demonstrated by the

97

liturgy, which, in celebrating on Holy Thursday the institution of the Eucharist, ever points out to us the cross; while adoring the cross on Good Friday, it salutes that cross as the tree of life planted for the cure of the whole world. . . .

The Last Supper taken by Christ with His disciples has had a twofold effect: a real action accomplished once for all; a ritual action ever renewable. The mystery is that the two are only one. First, the Last Supper inaugurated this supreme and saving event in human history: the voluntary passion of the God-Man. From this emerged the new creation which, by the cross once lifted above the world, suffices to renew all things. The Last Supper, too, begot that unlimited liturgical development that in so many places at all times, until the end of the world, should reproduce Christ's last banquet with His disciples, and, in this banquet, the sole oblation of the eternal sacrifice.

LOUIS BOUYER [86]

GOOD FRIDAY
THE PASSION AND DEATH OF THE LORD

If Holy Thursday can be called "the hour of Jesus," Good Friday will be "the hour of the prince of darkness": two hours that make but one; complementary aspects of the same, the most important, moment for the history of humanity, when God drew from sin its own remedy. The "hour of the prince of darkness" is the same as the "hour of Jesus," for the reason that our reconciliation with the Father, our victory over the enemy who held us chained to his revolt, demanded the immolation of the just One.

The Good Friday synaxis [service] will give us the meaning of this necessary immolation in enabling us to see in Christ the Servant of Yahveh foreseen by the prophets, the Victim Who, to take away the sins of the world, must begin by carrying their weight. But this synaxis will also show us in Him the eternal Priest of the new covenant prefigured by the old: the Priest Who alone renders fruitful the suffering and death of the fallen creature, for He alone can make of them the means of an efficacious sacrifice, can make of the cross the instrument of triumph, can make of a gibbet the tree of life. We, in a word, are

98

going to examine the mysterious necessity and the not less mysterious efficacy of suffering and death for redemption.

LOUIS BOUYER [87]

"Unlike any other day in the whole Christian year of the Occident, Good Friday has an aliturgical synaxis: that is, there is no celebration of the eucharistic sacrifice. There is indeed communion . . . but it is communion with the hosts consecrated the day before. In this fact the extraordinary character of Good Friday is set in relief: the Son of Man is no longer active except by a voluntary passivity. According to His own expression, He is *delivered to the wicked,* who do *unto Him whatsoever they have a mind.* [Mt. 17, 12]

This consummation of the sacrifice of the preceding day, however, prevents us from forgetting that, if the prince of this world is now having his hour, he can force his Victim to undergo nothing but what that Victim yesterday freely consented to undergo. Behind the "folly of the cross," the "wisdom of God," present in the very heart of darkness in order to draw light out of it, allows itself to be reached by faith. The sadness of Good Friday is then very real, but it is the *sadness according to God* which St. Paul has so carefully distinguished from *the sadness according to the world.* [2 Cor. 7, 8ff.] It is the sadness of compunction, that is, a sadness that implies hope. It is the sadness of the sinner conscious of this horror of his sin, at the thought of what it has cost the love of God to make atonement for it. . . .

This service includes four parts. The first, analogous to the vigil or the Mass of the Catechumens, but of primitive simplicity, is a succession of lessons and tracts. The second part is a series of prayers for the needs of the whole Church. The third is the solemn rite of the adoration of the cross. The last part is . . . communion with the hosts consecrated at the Holy Thursday Mass.

The prophecies and canticles, combined and culminating with the chanting of the Passion according to St. John, will unfold for us, in Christ, that Servant of Yahveh whom the last of the prophets had pictured: the Servant suffering and dying for the sins of Israel. In suffering for these sins, however, He cancels them. The great prayers will bring out this other aspect—the

99

sacerdotal one, of the Passion. Conforming to the doctrine of the Epistle to the Hebrews read at Tenebrae of this day, these prayers will reveal to us in Christ on the cross the High Priest of the new covenant, who, by a single oblation of Himself, has been able to offer in the celestial sanctuary His all-powerful intercession. After that, we shall adore the cross: no longer for us the simple instrument of the most odious of crimes, but the "tree of life planted for the cure of nations." The sadness of this cross has "brought joy to the world," according to the specific words of the liturgy. The General Communion will conclude the Good Friday service, consummating the sacrifice of Holy Thursday just as the death of Christ on the cross consummated the eucharistic service of the Upper Room.

LOUIS BOUYER [88]

And when upon our brows,
Each year,
The immortal Ash
Marks us for God;
May that mark,
Struck on the declarative face,
The written Sign
Of this night's grim
Agonization,
Purge us,
Make us a fit
Habitat
For the Bread
And for the Wine;
Renew us in the eternal Covenant,
Launched outward in His members
On His earthly quest.
Through Him,
Mankind broke out of History,
Who waited in the Virgin's womb
The nine ages of His knowledgeable gestation,
And walked on flaming feet,
And wrote the mark of liberation
Everywhere on the wondering human face.

Let the ignorant rooster
Riddle every sunrise with his cry.
No more have fear.
Advent is past.
Epiphany, its blazing
Declaration done.
The long Lent closes.
Before a new day drops
Man's terrible penance
Will be lifted from his back.

And now the night alarms.

Far off the posse
Gathers its torches up,
Unfolds
Its sullen plan.

Good Friday
Draws like a scalpel
On the mordant
Soul of man.

BROTHER ANTONINUS [89]

HOLY SATURDAY

The empty day.

The appearance of the church between the liturgy of Good Friday and the liturgy of Holy Saturday is extraordinary. Again the altar has been stripped of its linens. It remains bare. All the lights are extinguished. The empty tabernacle stands open. Only the image of the cross appears, unveiled; all bend the knee before it. The impression sought by the liturgy is certainly that of an absence. The tomb encloses the inanimate body of the Savior; the soul has gone to the abode of the dead.

The Oriental liturgies have a burial service in which the sorrow of sinful humanity in the presence of the death it has inflicted upon the God who saved it, was often expressed with poignant poetry. The Occidental liturgy is unacquainted with this service. The compunction awakened by the thought of what our salvation has cost our Savior seems still deeper when that sorrow is manifested simply by stripping the altars and by silence. Once the sacrifice is consummated, however, compunction is no longer the sentiment that must dominate.

When the choir gathers again in the church deserted by the divine Presence, and for the third and last time resumes the vigil of Tenebrae, the inevitable note of sadness will be touched by an inviolable peace. Death has ended suffering and sorrow for the crucified One, heart-rending and painful as they were. Henceforth "all," especially all suffering, is consummated. Presages of the Resurrection brighten Holy Saturday morning. From that very hour . . . we have been able to hymn the victory of the cross. The Church, quiet near the tomb of her Spouse, is already at peace. The repose of Christ is that of the second sabbath of God, following the work of the second creation, as the first sabbath had ended the first creation.

LOUIS BOUYER [90]

THE PASCHAL VIGIL

There are three essential parts in the "holy night." The first is the Lucernarium, the ancient prayer for the hour when lamps are lighted, a prayer that becomes on this day a canticle for the Resurrection and for the light with which it illumines the world. The second essential part of this "holy night" is the vigil, one so solemn, says Tertullian, that all Christians of his time were obliged to assist at it. Devoted to the final teaching of the catechumens, this vigil unfolds before us. . . . the Old Testament passages prophetic of Christ. The third part of the "holy night" observance not only celebrates but also renews the Savior's resurrection, by the baptism of the neophytes, or, at the very least (if no one presents himself), by the blessing of the water whereof will be born the sons of the divine Ichthus.* The synaxis ends

* This is a Greek word meaning "Fish." It is an anagram made up of the five initial letters of the five Greek words: *Iesous Christos,*

with the eucharistic banquet, of which the neophytes will partake for the first time with the faithful. The Alleluia will resound continuously at this point.

The vigil is marked by the extreme seriousness of a final catechesis (the oral instruction of the catechumens), but what splendid visions it unfolds! The feast of lights and the feast of water between which the vigil occurs are only a glorious jubilation. It is the most royal expression of that unearthly joy which must ever pervade the redeemed soul and the redeemed Church. St. John knew how to imprint it upon every page of the very book in which he described the tribulations that await the soul and the Church in this world until the *Parousia*. The Church, however, is not satisfied with merely reading the inspired word: she lives it and relives it day by day.

LOUIS BOUYER [91]

WE ARE EASTER MEN
AND ALLELUIA IS OUR SONG

Thus sang out St. Augustine. And time and time again, the timeless chant of Alleluia will ring out in our Christian churches this Easter season.

ALLELUIA—the word itself is Hebrew, a clear sign that it is an ancient song, ancient even when chanted by Jesus and his Apostles at their Passover meal, the night of his betrayal.

ALLELUIA—the meaning is "praise God." The Hebrew people had a whole series of psalms by that name that they used to sing at their most festive gatherings.

ALLELUIA, ALLELUIA—Praise the Lord God for making us a nation, praise Him for our national survival, praise to the God of Israel for being so closely involved in the history of his people!

But this Easter dawn, as we keep watch with the Church outside the empty tomb, the ancient Hebrew cry of wonder and thanks becomes our own—ALLELUIA, ALLELUIA, ALLELUIA! As sons of the Resurrection, we give praise in the face of the mystery of Christ.

Theou, Uios, Soter: Jesus Christ, Son of God, Savior. The fish symbol was much used by early Christians and particularly in connection with baptism.

He has risen! Death could not hold him! Now he lives no more to die!

At the Easter Vigil, the most solemn and important of all church services, we stand with lighted candles to renew the promises of our baptism. As the parish church is illumined by the light from the great Christ-candle, we realize that the risen Lord lives on in all who believe in him. We are aware that we have been transfigured by the light of his Resurrection.

Could this be possible? How could this mortal nature of ours come into contact with the person of the risen Christ? It is our holy faith (truly an Easter faith) that tells us that it is so. In loving gratitude we respond "praise God"—ALLELUIA!

In the Vigil Mass early this Easter morning (as in every Mass) we meet the risen Christ. We meet him just as truly as the Magdalene met him in the garden outside his tomb; we meet him as personally as Paul encountered him on the road to Damascus.

Christ has risen; he reigns in glory; he transcends the limits of time and space—yet in the liturgy we meet him.

It is this overwhelming fact of the Resurrection of Christ that colors the whole "good news" of our salvation. In St. Augustine's words, we are truly "Easter men." Our faith is based on the fact of Easter; our membership in Christ's glory rests upon our share in his rising by the sacrament of baptism; our Christian morality impels us to live the "risen life," a life worthy of a member of the Easter community.

EDWARD HOWARD [92]

EASTER EVE

O night more light than day,
more bright than the sun,
O night more white than snow,
more brilliant than many torches,
O night of more delight than is paradise.

Night devoid of all dark,
O night dispelling sleep
and teaching us the vigilance of angels,
O night the demons tremble at,
night of all nights in all the year desired.

Night of the Church's bridal,
night of new birth in baptism,
night when the Devil slept and was stripped,
night when the Heir took the heiress
to enjoy their inheritance.

ASTERIUS OF AMASIA [93]

ALLELUIA

This is the night on which you first caused our forefathers, the children of Israel, to pass dry-shod through the Red Sea as they escaped from Egypt.

This is the night on which, destroying the chains of death, Christ rose victoriously from the grave. For birth would have meant nothing to us if we had not been redeemed.

O wondrous condescension of your mercy toward us!

O incomprehensible goodness of love: to redeem a slave you delivered up your Son!

O truly necessary sin of Adam, deleted by the death of Christ!

O happy fault, that won for us a Redeemer so holy and so great!

O truly blessed night, which alone deserved to know the hour in which Christ rose from the grave!

PASCHAL VIGIL [94]

Paschal Time

The Jewish Passover celebrated the victorious outcome of the dramatic struggle between Moses, Yahweh's spokesman, and Pharaoh, representing the powers of this world. It required the blood of the immolated paschal lamb to free God's first-born, the people of Israel, from slavery, and to beat down, even momentarily, the proud obstinacy of Pharaoh who held out so stubbornly till vanquished by the death of his first-born son. Above all it took the intervention of the almighty power of God to save His people entrapped between the Egyptian troops and the sea. Then came the passage through the waters of the Red Sea, opening a path toward the Promised Land.[1] Still, forty years of wandering in the desert then preceded their entry into Chanaan under Joshua, once again dry-shod through water, that of the River Jordan this time. At Galgala, on the plain of Jericho, they celebrated the initial Passover after their entry into Chanaan, keeping holiday before the Lord to celebrate his rescuing mercy.[2]

The Exodus, the Forty Years, the Entry into the Land of Promise, dominated the religious life of the Israelites. But they were mere shadows of things to come; their reality is found in Christ.[3] He is the Lamb immolated to save His people from the slavery of sin;[4] He is the true First-born delivered from death by

[1] Introit of the Monday and Saturday of Easter Week; Offertory of Friday.
[2] Jos. 3, 14—5, 12.
[3] Col. 2, 17.
[4] Epistle and Communion of Easter Sunday.

106

the resurrection;[5] He is the true Joshua who leads the faithful into the true Land of Promise, the life of the Risen Christ, in which they participate already in this world, while awaiting plenary possession of it on the day of His glorious Return.[6]

During the forty days between Easter and the Ascension, Christ formed His apostles and disciples to live in His invisible but abiding presence. He no longer dwelt constantly with them but only appeared among them from time to time in transfigured fashion. They were to remember chiefly how He preferred to share their meals with them, thus continuing and strengthening the sacred fellowship of their earlier common meals and of the Last Supper. Little by little He accustomed them to find Him for the future in the gatherings of the Christian community, especially in the Lord's Supper. They had to learn to live in faith and in eschatological expectancy.

During Paschaltide the Church relives those early days of her apprenticeship. Waiting is over; Christ is risen; she does not have to look for the living among the dead. But each year she tries to renew her appreciation of her Lord's overwhelming triumph and total victory and to discover once again the riches deposited by the Savior in her care.

Risen with Christ she lingers contemplatively over the luminous scenes of His paschal appearances, trying to recapture the joyous strength which the apostles drew from these appearances[7] and which they communicated so vividly in their kerygmatic preaching.[8] She prefers, in particular, to contemplate the spectacle of the newly baptized, those who issued forth from her virginal womb on Easter Eve and in whom the Risen Savior now dwells. She tries to reveal to them what they have become: they now stand safe and sound on solid land like Noah upon quitting the ark[9] or like the Hebrew People deposited securely on the far side of the Red Sea; they have been rescued from Egyptian darkness—death and sin—by the victorious hand of God;[10] as a

[5] Introit and Collect of Easter Sunday.
[6] Collect of Easter Wednesday.
[7] Gospels of Easter Week.
[8] Epistles of Monday, Tuesday, and Wednesday.
[9] Friday's Epistle.
[10] Introit of Friday and Saturday.

new People of God chosen from among the Gentiles, they have drunk from the sources of living water; a chosen people, a royal priesthood, a holy nation, they have been called forth from darkness into the marvelous light of the Risen Christ.[11] The Church invites her neophytes to enjoy the sweetness of the Lord with the simplicity of little children[12] and to live in Christian unity by means of faith working through love. The living waters of Baptism have already quenched their thirst; now the Eucharist is to be their nourishing sustenance.[13] This sacrament of unity pours forth the love of Christ in their hearts and progressively transforms them into new creatures.[14] Although the Church addresses the newly baptized in the Easter liturgy, she does not forget her older members. During the Easter Vigil all present are asked to renew their baptismal vows in a formal way, and the whole of Eastertide is designed to remind them, too, of their baptismal commitment.[15]

There could be a danger, however, lurking in the midst of these paschal celebrations. Those seeking the things that are above[16] run the risk of neglecting "the terrible duties of every day" which belong to their Christian life on earth. The quest for holiness can distract us from the world; contemplation can deprive us of any taste for action; intense faith can cause us to despise earthly realities. When we fix our eyes too rigidly where true joys are to be found,[17] the splendors of paradise may blind us, making us forget the sufferings of men.

Very wisely the Church unceasingly reminds us that we must realize in our lives the holiness expressed in the sacred rites.[18] A reading of the Epistle of St. James should dissipate any illusion on this score: we must be doers and not just hearers of the Word.[19]

[11] Saturday's Epistle.
[12] Introit of Low Sunday.
[13] Wednesday's Prayer over the Offerings (*Secreta*).
[14] Wednesday's Postcommunion.
[15] Friday's Offertory.
[16] Tuesday's Communion.
[17] Collect of the Fourth Sunday after Easter.
[18] Collect, Friday of Easter Week.
[19] Epistles, Fourth and Fifth Sundays after Easter.

The Gospels of the last Sundays after Easter, taken from Jesus' final discourse after the Last Supper, depict for us the vocation of the Christian living in the world but not of the world.[20] Jesus bequeathed these precious instructions to us for our illumination and direction after the withdrawal of His visible presence. We disciples are summoned to be worthy of our Master now in glory. Christ has introduced us to the Father and our intimate union with Him is to become the springing source of love uniting us both to God and men.

Christ can ascend into heaven confident that the work His Father gave Him has been accomplished.[21] No doubt His apostles await and expect His return, but in the meantime His Spirit will teach them all things and transform them and the world as He broods over the new creation.[22] The time of apprenticeship in the faith is over. Now is the time for building up the Mystical Body of Christ which lives by His spirit.[23] His members can actively prepare for the mission entrusted to them by their Lord, the mission of preaching the Good News to the whole world.[24] The history of the Church now begins.

EASTER SUNDAY

This is the day which the Lord has made: let us be glad and rejoice! (Gradual)

Let us celebrate this feast, the greatest of all the feasts, a feast of light, the Resurrection of the Lord! Let us celebrate together, in joy and piety, because the Lord has been raised and he has raised the whole world with him. Rising he has broken the chains of death. Adam sinned, Adam is dead. Christ did not sin and yet he died. What a strange anomaly: Adam sinned and died; Christ did not sin and died. Why? So that he who died for having sinned

[20] Jn. 16, 5-30; Vigil of the Ascension and Sixth Sunday after Easter (Jn. 17, 1-11; 15, 26-27; 16, 1-4).
[21] Gospel, Vigil of the Ascension.
[22] Gospel, Sixth Sunday after Easter.
[23] Epistle, Vigil of the Ascension.
[24] Gospel, Ascension Thursday.

could be freed from the chains of death by him who died
without having sinned.

ST. JOHN CHRYSOSTOM [95]

EASTER HYMN

This is the paschal feast, the Lord's passing:
so cries the Spirit.
No type or telling, this,
no shadow;
Pasch of the Lord it is, and truly.
The blood that is shed is a sign of the blood to be shed,
the first indication of what the Spirit will be,
a glimpse of the great anointing.
I, seeing the blood, will protect you.

You have indeed protected us, Jesus,
from endless disaster.
You spread your hands like a Father
and fatherlike gave cover with your wings.
Your blood, a God's blood, you poured over the earth,
sealing a blood-bargain
for men because you loved them.
What anger threatened you turned away from us;
instead you gave us back God's friendship.

The heavens may have your spirit, paradise your soul,
but O may the earth have your blood.

This feast of the Spirit
leads the mystic dance through the year.
The pasch came from God, came from heaven to earth;
from earth it has gone back to heaven.
New is this feast and all-embracing;
all creation assembles at it.

Joy to all creatures, honour, feasting, delight.
Dark death is destroyed
and life is restored everywhere.
The gates of heaven are open.

God has shown himself man,
man has gone up to him a God.
The gates of hell God has shattered,
the bars of Adam's prison broken.
The people of the world below have risen from the dead,
bringing good news:
what was promised is fulfilled.
From the earth has come singing and dancing.

This is God's passing.
Heaven's God, showing no meanness,
has joined us to himself in the Spirit.
The great marriage-hall is full of guests,
all dressed for the wedding, no guest rejected
for want of a wedding-dress.
The paschal light is the bright new lamp-light,
light that shines from the virgins' lamps.
The light in the soul will never go out.
The fire of grace burns in us all,
spirit, divine,
in our bodies and in our souls,
fed with the oil of Christ.

We pray you, God, our Sovereign, Christ,
King for ever in the world of spirits,
stretch out your strong hands over your holy Church
and over the people that will always be yours.
Defend, protect, preserve them,
fight and do battle for them,
subject their enemies to them,
subdue the invisible powers that oppose them,
as you have already subdued those that hate us.
Raise now the sign of victory over us
and grant
that we may sing with Moses the song of triumph.
For yours are victory and power
for ever and ever. Amen.

ST. HIPPOLYTUS OF ROME [96]

111

Christ conquers, Christ reigns, Christ rules.

What was Christ doing in His Passion? Christ went down into death. He went where death is master. He put Himself into death's hands. The lower parts of the earth—the phrase does not simply mean the tomb, but also the lower regions, and in Greek theology the Resurrection was not simply Christ coming out of the tomb, but Christ coming up from hell. The notion is not the same—and the theological implications are far deeper. Christ went down into the domain of death, to that manhood which was under death's dominion, and there was a moment when death could cry "I am the victor." To which St. Paul gave that magnificent answer: *Oh death, where is thy victory?* [1 Cor. 15, 55]. Death, whose name is Satan, thought on Good Friday to be forever victorious, for Christ Himself was its prisoner. And then, on Easter morning, the gate burst, the prisons of death were opened up: *O death, where is thy victory?*

Christ could not conquer death in this particular way without first becoming its prisoner. He fell into its power to set mankind free. And this gives His death an incomparable realism, and an incomparable grandeur, and gives the word *Redemption* its fullest meaning. It was not simply a buying back, squaring of an account between Christ and Satan, but Christ's struggle against the powers of evil, and His victory over them all and over the dominion of death. This explains the rites of baptism as practiced in the Early Church. The descent into the baptismal pool, which St. Paul connects with the burial of Christ, symbolized this going down into death. The newly baptized were incorporated into Christ's death before emerging victorious with Him.

That victory of Christ's holds good for all men. Every man should reproduce in himself the whole mystery of Christ—His Passion, Resurrection, and Ascension—and baptism is a symbol of that conformity with Christ which is to be carried on throughout life. Christ's victory over the powers of evil is completed in us through mortification and the final liberation it brings.

JEAN DANIELOU [97]

112

MONDAY WITHIN THE OCTAVE OF EASTER

In the Gospel we are told how two disciples were going to Emmaus, burning with love for Jesus and speaking of Him, when He appeared to them in the guise of a pilgrim, and taught them how the prophecies of Scripture applied to Himself. *He opened their minds to understand the meaning of the Scriptures* [Lk. 24: 45]. In the same way the spiritual presence of Jesus opens the minds of those who love Him and burn with desire for Him. Through the ministry of the angels it brings the words and teachings of Holy Scripture to their minds without effort and study, and reveals their meaning, however difficult or obscure. Indeed, the more difficult and remote from human understanding they are, the greater the joy of the soul when their true meaning is revealed to it by God Himself. And if the words permit it, they are interpreted both in a literal, moral, mystical, and heavenly sense. By the literal interpretation, which is the simplest and most direct, man's natural intelligence is satisfied. By the moral interpretation of Scripture the soul is taught about virtues and vices, and enabled to distinguish between them. By the mystical interpretation the soul is illumined to recognize God's workings within His Church, and to apply the words of Scripture to Christ our Head, and to His mystical body, the Church. The fourth, or heavenly, interpretation refers solely to the activity of love, and attributes all the truths of Scripture to the workings of love. And since this corresponds most closely to the experience of heaven, I call it heavenly.

One who loves God is His friend, not because he has deserved this privilege, but because God in His merciful goodness takes him as His friend with a solemn pledge. He reveals His secrets to him, and treats him as a true friend who pleases and loves Him, and does not merely serve Him with fear like a slave. Thus Jesus Himself says to His Apostles: *I now call you My friends, for I make known to you all that I have heard from My Father.* [Jn. 15, 15] To a pure soul, whose palate is cleansed from the corruption of worldly love, Holy Scripture is nourishing food and delicious sustenance. Its taste is wonderfully sweet when fully assimilated by the understanding, for within it is concealed the life-

giving spirit which quickens all the powers of the soul, and fills
them with heavenly sweetness and spiritual delight.

WALTER HILTON [98]

Did not our hearts burn with us as he opened to us the Scriptures.
(Gospel)

Drink of Christ as you drink of His words.
His word is the Old Testament,
and His word is the New Testament.
The divine Scriptures are imbibed and eaten
when the rich nourishment of the eternal Word
comes into the inner recesses of
our mind and heart.

ST. AMBROSE [99]

They knew him in the breaking of bread. (Gospel)

The notion of encounter with Christ, of movement to Christ,
reaches its greatest and most unique intensity in the sacrament
of the Eucharist. The glorified Lord himself comes to us in bodily
form. Let us consider this encounter in the Mass.

F. X. Durrwell . . . speaks of the Mass: "The breaking of
bread among the disciples at the Last Supper made it possible for
the experience of the presence of the risen Lord to endure through
time. Historically speaking, this is the first explanation of the
meaning of the Mass: The Lord is alive and present among his disciples who have gathered together for the breaking of bread."
This explanation remains the first one for us also. All instruction
and preaching on the Mass should begin with the notion of the
presence of the Lord. The point must be stressed that the Lord
who was glorified because of his passion and death wishes to
enter our gathering today. He desires to eat the supper with us.
Once this initial explanation of the Mass has been grasped, one
can then unveil the deepest significance of the mystery of the
Mass: the sacrifice of the cross which takes place, here and now,
among us.

Viewing the celebration of the Eucharist as an encounter
with the risen Lord, two highpoints are discernible. The first oc-

curs at the Gospel. All the various prayers which precede the actual eucharistic celebration converge toward this first meeting with Christ in the Gospel. The Lord comes into the assembly in the form of his word. The people greet him with the response, "Glory to thee, O Lord." The second highpoint of the encounter occurs at the Consecration and Communion, when the people meet Christ himself corporally in the Eucharist.

This theme of encounter with the risen Lord in the Mass strongly influenced eucharistic piety in the early centuries. The response of the people, "We have lifted our hearts to the Lord," recited in the Preface of the Mass, was often understood as a reference to the glorified Christ. Indeed, one might say that this response is the leitmotif of the whole framework of the liturgy in which we meet Christ. The Church and all her members lift up their hearts to the glorified man Jesus who approaches them in the liturgy.

BALTHASAR FISCHER [100]

TUESDAY WITHIN THE OCTAVE OF EASTER

The proclamation of Christ's death and the resurrection was made *first of all,* both in point of time, and in point of importance and effectiveness, by the celebration of the Eucharist. This proclamation was and is the root of all Christian teaching and preaching. *Proclaiming the death of the Lord* [1 Cor. 11, 26] by doing and saying what Christ did and said at the Last Supper is the seed, the source, the summary of the whole of Christian catechetics. The entire body of New Testament writings is no more than its unfolding, under the impulse of the Spirit. The Gospels and Epistles, which from earliest times were read at the Eucharistic gathering are a broader statement, a more detailed declaration, a framework of the central mystery of our Lord's saving death and resurrection which is performed and proclaimed by the words of Institution: *This is My body which shall be given for you; this cup is the new covenant in My blood.* [1 Cor. 11, 25]

This proclamation is heart and center of all proclamation. Even if (to cite an extreme hypothesis) there had been no Scriptures of the New Testament, even if the truths of our faith had

115

never been formulated in official creeds, even if no pope or general council had in the course of history made a pronouncement about the data of revelation, the central mystery of our faith would still have been substantially proclaimed to the world by the celebration of holy Mass.

So far as the life and the faith of the new people of God is concerned, it is not creed, or catechism, or council—it is the proclamation of the death and resurrection of our Lord by the celebration of the Eucharist that is primary and most basic. It is by the pronouncing of the Eucharistic Prayer that the Church most solemnly, most eloquently, most effectively proclaims her faith in the saving death and resurrection of Christ until He comes.

GODFREY DIEKMANN [101]

He opened their minds to understand the Scriptures. (Gospel)

On the sacred and blessed altar we behold two particularly precious and venerable objects, a Book and a Chalice. This is the task that is called to mind by the Book laid open upon the altar: to teach true doctrine, proper discipline of life, and the ways in which man can rise toward God. Alongside the Book stands the Chalice. The most sacred and most mysterious part of the Eucharistic liturgy centers around the Chalice of Jesus. There is no perfection in Christian life or practice aside from participation in the Eucharistic banquet.

JOHN XXIII [102]

WEDNESDAY WITHIN THE OCTAVE OF EASTER

Jesus appeared to the disciples after he had risen from the dead. (Gospel)

Christ did not merely announce the resurrection. He brought it. In his own resurrection he inaugurated and made possible the resurrection of mankind. Today we usually consider Christ's resurrection as coming after the gospel as its seal and confirmation.

However, in primitive Christianity the resurrection was the central affirmation of the gospel. The resurrection brought the Messianic age; it was the vindication and exaltation of Christ. Through the risen Christ came the outpouring of the life-giving Spirit.

In proclaiming the resurrection of Christ, the apostles announced our resurrection in him. His resurrection and exaltation were the certain pledge of his second coming in glory to establish his kingdom and to raise the dead. The impatient expectation of this return, the Parousia, constituted the eschatological hope of the first Christians which is preserved intact in the theologies of Paul and John.

CHARLES DAVIS [103]

In a movement of supreme love for his creature, God decides to save man. Among all the means, he chooses the one that testifies to his most ardent love and regard for man. For he wants man, in a certain sense, to save himself. Hence, God sends his only Son to become one of us. Christ is the first one to make this return to the Father. He, remaining sinless, passes from the condition of a sinner to the divine friendship. As St. John says, *He passes from this world to his Father.* [Jn. 13, 1]

This return of man to God is not effected by a kind of juridical fiction, nor solely by a reparation of a purely moral order. The return consists essentially in the fact that Christ took upon himself the likeness of a sinful flesh, without himself becoming a sinner, and he died to that flesh to rise again with a glorified body, becoming a "life-giving spirit."

But Christ was not simply the first to return to God. In a certain way, all men return with him. Our participation in his death and resurrection through baptism presupposes that Christ, in rising from the dead, brought with him all those who are called one day to participate in this mystery. The Judaic notion of first fruits suggests this solidarity. In the first fruits is contained the whole harvest. To express the unique solidarity between Christ and all Christians, Paul was able to declare with no fear of being misunderstood: *For just as the body is one and yet has many parts, so it is with Christ; . . . you are a body which is Christ.* [1 Cor. 12, 12. 27].

117

Restored to God in Christ, each Christian, as a free being, must participate in this restoration by a personal act of his freedom, and thus, in his turn, must die and rise again. This personal return is accomplished by faith and baptism. Thus each one of us passes from the earthly to the spiritual life, from the city of evil built by self-love, to the city of God built by divine love.

Viewed as the supreme act of love and obedience, Christ's death and resurrection, far from being opposed, are actually more closely linked together; death already implies the resurrection. Christ's act of love, since it is God's own act, cannot help but be sovereignly efficacious, essentially vivifying, communicating life first of all to his own human nature, and then to every human nature incorporated into him by baptism.

The death and resurrection are simply two aspects of one unique mystery, somewhat analogous to the twofold aspect of justification—the remission of sins and the infusion of sanctifying grace. As the paschal liturgy recalls, within the passion and death shines the victory of the resurrection, and in the risen Christ there remain the vestiges of his passion and death.

STANISLAS LYONNET [104]

THURSDAY WITHIN THE OCTAVE OF EASTER

Do you understand what you are reading? (Lesson I)

In the Apocalypse, a book sealed with seven seals is exhibited. If you give this book to an educated person and suggest he read it, he will reply, "Impossible, this book is sealed." How many there are today who imagine themselves to be cultured yet the Bible to them is a sealed book! They cannot open it unless He unlocks it Who possesses David's key, for "when he opens it no man can shut it, and when he shuts it no man can open it." One remembers the holy eunuch in the Acts of the Apostles—or rather, the "pious man" as Scripture designates him—was reading Isaiah when Philip questioned, *Do you grasp what you read? How can I,* replied the eunuch, *unless some man show me?* To digress for a moment. Holier or more studious than the

118

eunuch I am not. He had come from Ethiopia, the very ends of the earth, leaving behind a queen's palace in order to visit the Temple at Jerusalem; and such a lover of divine wisdom he was that he even read the Sacred Writings while riding in his chariot. Yet, though he grasped the Bible in his hands, taking into his very thoughts the Lord's words so that they were on the tip of his tongue, still he failed to realize Who it was he venerated in such an unenlightened fashion. Philip came and showed him Jesus Who was concealed behind the words on the page. What a miraculous, what a virtuous teacher! In that same hour the eunuch believed, and was baptized; he became one of the faithful and, later, a saint, no longer a pupil but a teacher. This eunuch discovered more in that church fountain in the desert than he had ever found in the glittering Temple of the synagogue.

ST. JEROME [105]

FRIDAY WITHIN THE OCTAVE OF EASTER

Teach all nations! (Gospel)

Come, help us now! While in preceding ages the hierarchy arrogated the ministry completely to itself, today it calls on the laity to collaborate by its side . . . The day is growing late. It is necessary to work today, immediately, that not an hour be lost. The needs are immense and urgent. Come, help us tell the world where truth is and where error is—this world so distracted and almost overcome by centrifugal movements. The layman is one of the major hopes of the Church. Now is the hour of the laity.

PAUL VI [106]

In our times we cannot recommend higher values to people by making speeches about them. People—to put it very bluntly—have had their bellyfull of our sermonizing. They are seeking a source of strength for their lives; they want a sense and a meaning that will give them this strength. The higher values and vital strength can be recommended to others only by making

119

them actively present in ourselves. Contact with Christians must be an experience which proves to men that Christianity is a power transforming the whole of life. Through Amos his prophet God makes a reproach that could very often be laid at our door: *If you offer me holocausts and your gifts, I will not receive them. . . . Take away from me the tumult of your songs: and I will not hear the canticles of your harp. But let judgment flow as water, and justice as a mighty torrent.* [Am. 5, 22–25] Our existence and activity as Christians in the world is very often a dilution of the true visibility of a life redeemed in Christ. And in this, the very thing we minimize, we should recognize the rightful position of the laity, indeed of all believers, in the Church. We may go to Church on Sunday and abstain from meat on Friday—well and good—but we are still a long way from having made holiness a reality in the midst of this world. And until we do, we are obscuring the sign that the Church should be to all the world.

We must show a real love for our fellow men, and this love must truly be the sacrament of our love for God. But this sacramentality in its turn has an effect upon our human love for our fellow men, for however much we as believers can and should share the problems of unbelievers in order to retain side by side with them a solidarity in human experience, we cannot share their lack of redemption. A Christian's *présence au monde*, which is the great motive of credibility for the Christian faith, is always motivated by redemption. The Christian lives in the world because he lives in and with the living God; his is a redeeming presence.

EDWARD SCHILLEBEECKX [107]

SATURDAY AFTER EASTER

The royal priesthood. (Epistle)

Mother Church earnestly desires that all the faithful should be led to that full, conscious, and active participation in liturgical celebrations which is demanded by the very nature of the liturgy.

Such participation by the Christian people as *a chosen race, a royal priesthood, a holy nation, a redeemed people* [1 Pet. 2, 9], is their right and duty by reason of their baptism.

In the restoration and promotion of the sacred liturgy, this full and active participation by all the people is the aim to be considered before all else; for it is the primary and indispensable source from which the faithful are to derive the true Christian spirit; and therefore pastors of souls must zealously strive to achieve it, by means of the necessary instruction, in all their pastoral work.

CONSTITUTION ON THE SACRED LITURGY [108]

Alleluia!

Since it has pleased the Lord our God that, meeting here in person, we should, in union with your Charity, sing in His honor the "Alleluia" which is translated as "Praise God," let us give praise to the Lord, my brethren, in life and in speech, in heart and in voice, in words and in actions. For God wishes the "Alleluia" to be said in His honor in such a way that there will be nothing discordant in the one giving praise. Therefore, in ourselves above all let speech accord with life, tongue with conscience. I repeat, let our words agree with our actions lest, perhaps, fair words bear testimony against foul manners. O! joyous is the "Alleluia" in heaven where angels are the temple of God! For the utmost harmony of those giving praise exists there where there is tranquil rejoicing among those singing, where no law in the members opposes the law of the mind, where there is no conflict of desires in which the victory of charity is endangered. Here, therefore, let us sing "Alleluia" though we are still beset with cares, so that in the future we may sing it there in tranquillity.

ST. AUGUSTINE [109]

LOW SUNDAY

A HYMN TO CHRIST THE SAVIOUR

I

Bridle of colts untamed,
  Over our wills presiding;
Wing of unwandering birds,
  Our flight securely guiding.
Rudder of youth unbending,
  Firm against adverse shock;
Shepherd, with wisdom tending
  Lambs of the royal flock
Thy simple children bring
In one, that they may sing
In solemn lays
Their hymns of praise
With guileless lips to Christ their King.

II

King of saints, almighty Word
Of the Father highest Lord;
Wisdom's head and chief;
Assuagement of all grief;
Lord of all time and space,
Jesus, Saviour of our race;
Shepherd, who dost us keep;
  Husbandman, who tillest,
Bit to restrain us, Rudder
  To guide us as Thou willest;
Of the all-holy flock celestial wing;
Fisher of men, whom Thou to life dost bring;
  From evil sea of sin,
    And from the billowy strife,
  Gathering pure fishes in,
    Caught with sweet bait of life:
  Lead us, Shepherd of the sheep,
    Reason-gifted, holy One;

King of youths, whom Thou dost keep,
  So that they pollution shun:
Steps of Christ, celestial Way;
  Word eternal, Age unending;
Life that never can decay;
  Fount of mercy, virtue-sending;
Life august of those who raise
Unto God their hymn of praise,
                    Jesus Christ!

III

Nourished by the milk of heaven,
To our tender palates given;
Milk of wisdom from the breast
Of that bride of grace exprest;
By a dewy spirit filled
From fair Reason's breast distilled;
Let us sucklings join to raise
With pure lips our hymns of praise
As our grateful offering,
Clean and pure, to Christ our King.
Let us, with hearts undefiled,
Celebrate the mighty Child.
We, Christ-born, the choir of peace;
  We, the people of His love.
Let us sing, nor ever cease,
  To the God of peace above.

ST. CLEMENT OF ALEXANDRIA [110]

SECOND SUNDAY AFTER EASTER

Christ suffered for us, leaving you an example that you should follow in his footsteps. (Epistle)

Grant now, O blessed [martyrs designate], that even to Christians the prison is unpleasant. But we were called to the warfare of the living God in our very response to the sacramental words.

123

Well, no soldier comes out to the campaign laden with luxuries, nor does he go to action from his comfortable chamber, but from the light and narrow tent, where every kind of hardness and roughness and disagreeableness must be put up with. Even in peace soldiers inure themselves to war by toils and inconveniences—marching in arms, running over the plain, working at the ditch, making the *testudo,* engaging in many arduous labours. The sweat of the brow is in everything, that bodies and minds may not shrink at having to pass from shade to sunshine, from sunshine to icy cold, from the robe of peace to the coat of mail, from silence to clamour, from quiet to tumult. In like manner, O blessed, count whatever is hard in this lot of yours as a discipline of your powers of mind and body. You are about to pass through a noble struggle, in which the living God acts the part of superintendent, in which the Holy Ghost is your trainer, in which the prize is an eternal crown of angelic essence, citizenship in the heavens, glory everlasting. Therefore your Master, Jesus Christ, who has anointed you with His Spirit, and led you forth to the arena, has seen it good, before the day of conflict, to take you from a condition more pleasant in itself, and imposed on you a harder treatment, that your strength might be the greater. For the athletes, too, are set apart to a more stringent discipline, that they may have their physical powers built up. They are kept from luxury, from daintier meats, from more pleasant drinks; they are pressed, racked, worn out; the harder their labours in the preparatory training, the stronger is the hope of victory. *And they,* says the Apostle, *that they may obtain a corruptible crown.* [1 Cor. 9, 25] We, with the crown eternal in our eye, look upon the prison as our training-ground, that at the goal of final judgment we may be brought forth well disciplined by many a trial; since virtue is built up by hardships, as by voluptuous indulgence it is overthrown.

TERTULLIAN [111]

I am the Good Shepherd. (Gospel)

It was in giving his life on the cross and in rising again from the dead that he proved himself to be, in a very special sense, the Good Shepherd. By these acts, he tackled the problem of man's misery at the very root. By dying, he conquered sin and took away man's death. By rising again, he brought mankind to the fullness of new life. In this new life human nature attains to that fruitfulness, bliss, and manifest fullness to which every community aspires as its ultimate perfection. It was the task of the shepherds of the people to aim at bringing about this perfection, but only the one genuinely Good Shepherd could achieve it. His resurrection, therefore, is first and foremost a great sign—a sign that he is indeed the Good Shepherd, and a sign of what he as Good Shepherd can and will accomplish. Those who take no cognizance of the resurrection in their appraisal of Christ the Good Shepherd, are left with no alternative but to put him on the level of any other public benefactor. To think of him as a good shepherd at all becomes pure sentimentality. And not only that; without the resurrection and it consequences for mankind, there is no comfort whatsoever in the image of the Good Shepherd. It is quite worthless.

JOHANNES PINSK [112]

THIRD SUNDAY AFTER EASTER

Grant that we who claim the name of Christian may . . . embrace all that enhances it. (Collect)

Let us not flatter ourselves in the mere fact that we are called Christians; rather, let us believe that we deserve to be judged if we assume a name to which we have no claim. Or, if anyone is so unbelieving, so unfaithful, so persistent, so obstinate, so bold, that he does not fear the imminent anger and indignation of God the judge, let him at least feel abashed before human judgments. Let him realize how dull, how foolish, and how senseless he is considered even by other people, since his vanity and madness are so great that he takes upon himself a name to which he is not entitled. For, who is so conceited and so pitiable that he would dare to establish himself as a lawyer if he is uneducated? Who is so mad and bereft of reason that he would proclaim himself a soldier if he does not know how to use arms? One does not choose such a name without reason. To be called a cobbler, one must repair shoes; to be looked upon as an artisan or workman, one must produce proof of his art; to be recognized as a trader, one exhibits costly objects originally purchased at a smaller price. From examples of this sort we realize that there is no name without the corresponding act and, furthermore, that every name is derived from the antecedent act. Now, then, are you called a Christian when you perform no distinctively Christian acts? The name Christian connotes justice, goodness, integrity, patience, chastity, prudence, humility, kindliness, innocence and piety; how do you defend your assumption of that name when your conduct manifests so few out of so many virtues? He is truly a Christian who is one not in name only but also in deed; who imitates and follows Christ in all respects; who is holy, innocent, undefiled, chaste; in whose heart evil finds no room, since this heart is dominated by piety and by a goodness which, knowing only how to bring help to all, knows not how to harm or injure anybody. He is a Christian who, according to the example of Christ, is accustomed to do good to those who oppose him and to pray for his persecutors and his enemies rather than to hate them. Whoever is quick to hurt or harm another person lies when he calls himself a Christian; he is truly a Christian who can say in all honesty: "I have harmed nobody; I have lived in justice with all men."

ST. AUGUSTINE [113]

The Christian way of life.

We are a body knit together as such by a common religious profession, by unity of discipline, and by the bond of a common hope. We meet together as an assembly and congregation, that, offering up prayer to God as with united force, we may wrestle with Him in our supplications. This violence God delights in. We pray, too, for the emperors, for their ministers and for all in authority, for the welfare of the world, for the prevalence of peace, for the delay of the final consummation. We assemble to read our sacred writings, if any peculiarity of the times makes

126

either forewarning or reminiscence needful. However it be in that respect with the sacred words, we nourish our faith, we animate our hope, we make our confidence more steadfast; and no less by inculcations of God's precepts we confirm good habits. In the same place also exhortations are made, rebukes and sacred censures are administered. For with a great gravity is the work of judging carried on among us, as befits those who feel assured that they are in the sight of God; and you have the most notable example of judgment to come when any one has sinned so grievously as to require his severance from us in prayer, and the meeting, and all sacred intercourse. The tried men of our elders preside over us, obtaining that honour not by purchase, but by established character. There is no buying and selling of any sort in the things of God. Though we have our treasure-chest, it is not made up of purchase-money, as of a religion that has its price. On the monthly collection day, if he likes, each puts in a small donation; but only if it be his pleasure, and only if he be able: for there is no compulsion; all is voluntary. These gifts are, as it were, piety's deposit fund. For they are not taken thence and spent on feasts, and drinking-bouts, and eating-houses, but to support and bury poor people, to supply the wants of boys and girls destitute of means and parents, and of old persons confined now to the house; such, too, as have suffered shipwreck; and if there happen to be any in the mines, or banished to the islands, or shut up in the prisons, for nothing but their fidelity to the cause of God's church, they become the nurslings of their confession. But it is mainly the deeds of a love so noble that lead many to put a brand upon us. See, they say, how they love one another, for they themselves are animated by mutual hatred; how they are ready even to die for one another, for they themselves will sooner put to death. And they are wroth with us, too, because we call each other brethren; for no other reason, as I think, than because among themselves names of consanguinity are assumed in mere pretence of affection. But we are your brethren as well, by the law of our common mother nature, though you are hardly men, because brothers so unkind. At the same time, how much more fittingly they are called and counted brothers who have been led to the knowledge of God as their common Father, who have drunk in one spirit of holiness, who from the same womb of a common ignorance have agonized into the same light of truth! But on this very account, perhaps, we are regarded as having less claim to be held true brothers, that no tragedy makes a noise about our brotherhood, or that the family possessions, which generally destroy brotherhood among you, create fraternal bonds among us. One in mind and soul, we do not hesitate to share our earthly goods with one another. All things are common among us but our wives.

TERTULLIAN [114]

FOURTH SUNDAY AFTER EASTER

It is expedient for you that I go away. (Gospel)

Whoso has a mind to know the excellence and use of absolute detachment let him lay to heart Christ's words to his disciples touching his manhood: *It is good for you that I go away; if I go not away the comforter cannot come unto you;* as though to say, you have too much love for my visible form for the perfect love of the Holy Ghost to be yours. Wherefore discard the form and unite with the formless essence, for God's ghostly comfort is intangible and is not offered save to those alone who despise all mortal consolations.

Listen, good people all: there is none happier than he who stands in uttermost detachment. No temporal, carnal pleasure but brings some ghostly mischief in its train, for the flesh lusts after things that run counter to the spirit and spirit lusts for things that are repugnant to the flesh. He who sows the tares of love in flesh reaps death but he who sows good love-seed in the spirit reaps of the spirit eternal life. The more man flees from creatures the faster hastens to him their creator. Consider, all you thoughtful souls! If even the love which it is given us to feel for the bodily form of Christ can keep us from receiving the Holy Ghost then how much more must we be kept from getting God by inordinate love of creature comforts? Detachment is the best of all, for it cleanses the soul, clarifies the mind, kindles the heart and wakes the spirit; it quickens desire and enhances virtue giving intuition of God; it detaches creature and makes her one with God; for love disjoined from God is as water in the fire, but love in union is like the honeycomb in honey. Listen, all rational souls! The swiftest steed to bear you to your goal is suffering; none shall ever taste eternal bliss but those who stand with Christ in depths of bitterness. Nothing is more gall-bitter than suffering, nothing so honey-sweet as to have suffered. The most sure foundation for this perfection is humility, for he whose nature here creeps in deepest depths shall soar in spirit to highest height of Deity; for joy brings sorrow and sorrow brings joy.

JOHN ECKHART [115]

When the Spirit of truth has come, he will teach you all the truth. (Gospel)

That Gift is the Spirit of God—in fact the "Spirit of Jesus"—through whom our hearts are filled with charity. No one, strictly speaking, knows God unless it be God alone. The Spirit enables us to know him in a certain measure, because it assimilates us to him. . . . The Spirit alone can plumb the depths of God. The Spirit alone grants us a knowledge of God which is more than radically inadequate or purely negative knowledge. The Spirit makes new men of us, men participating in the divine nature, as the Second Epistle of St. Peter makes bold to say, and gives us the only knowledge of God which is on his own level, because it is a connatural knowledge.

But this does not mean that the natural laws of the intelligence are suspended. The increase in knowledge obtained in this manner is not of a rational or philosophical order. It is something more or something else: but however that may be, it is different. It is not the privilege of the scholar or the reasoner. It is a knowledge related to experience. Or rather, it is worthless apart from that experience—which is wholly spiritual and beyond the reach of psychology. In one respect it is the privilege of that personal intimacy and concrete intuition which belongs to all religious knowledge, but in another respect it participates in its extra-scientific character. It is a simple, quasi-immediate knowledge, although in reality it is always analogical, *in speculo.* For

129

he who loves, St. John says, *is born of God, and knows God.*
[1 Jn. 4, 7] "He who loves," Augustine comments, "sees love,
and he who sees love sees God": *inde videmus, unde similes
sumus* (there we see where we are like); and this love, adds William of Saint-Thierry, is the eye which enables us to see God:
ipsa caritas enim est oculus quo videtur Deus. But at the same
time, that knowledge is precarious and always obscure, for it
depends upon a life which is both precarious and full of "vicis-
situdes," and never possessed as one possesses a natural good;
and because it can never catch the pure light which is shed by
that life, in the prism of the concept—and indeed never attempts
to do so.

HENRI DE LUBAC [116]

FIFTH SUNDAY AFTER EASTER

Religion that is pure and undefiled before God. (Epistle)

Let us, then, be "catholic." Let us open our eyes to the world and
our hearts to the love of all men. Let us at last understand
the demands of charity which, by its very essence, is catholic,
that is to say universal.

This is a difficult enough virtue—but Christ never pretended
that it would be easy to be His disciple.

A charity that is truly universal demands so many interior
renouncements and a willingness to impose upon oneself so many
material inconveniences! It is not easy to overcome natural re-
pugnance and all our antipathies, to silence all rancour, to forgive everything, to love truly and sincerely; to shake off apathy
and indifference, to conquer selfishness and love of ease and comfort; to sacrifice one's likes and dislikes; to give of one's time
and one's surplus means; to be friendly towards all, to be always
smiling; to be prepared to take risks, to forget oneself and to
give oneself. Often it requires a great strength of soul, and sometimes even heroism.

M. COUDRAY [117]

Ask in my name. (Gospel)

These considerations may serve to impress upon our minds the meaning of the precept in the text, and others like it which are found in St. Paul's Epistles. For instance, he enjoins the Ephesians to *pray always with all prayer and supplication in the Spirit.* [6, 18] To the Philippians he says, *Be careful for nothing; but in every thing by prayer and supplication let your requests be made known unto God.* [4, 6] To the Colossians, *Continue in prayer, and watch in the same with thanksgiving.* [4, 2] To the Romans, *Continue instant in prayer.* [12, 12]

Thus the true Christian pierces through the veil of this world and sees the next. He holds intercourse with it; he addresses God, as a child might address his parent, with as clear a view of Him, and with as unmixed a confidence in Him; with deep reverence indeed, and godly fear and awe, but still with certainty and exactness: as St. Paul says, *I know whom I have believed* [2 Tim. 1, 12], with the prospect of judgment to come to sober him, and the assurance of present grace to cheer him.

If what I have said is true, surely it is well worth thinking about. Most men indeed, I fear, neither pray at fixed times, nor do they cultivate an habitual communion with Almighty God. Indeed, it is too plain how most men pray. They pray now and then, when they feel particular need of God's assistance; when they are in trouble or in apprehension of danger; or when their feelings are unusually excited. They do not know what it is either to be habitually religious, or to devote a certain number of minutes at fixed times to the thought of God. Nay, the very best Christian, how lamentably deficient is he in the spirit of prayer! Let any man compare in his mind how many times he has prayed when in trouble, with how seldom he has returned thanks when his prayers have been granted; or the earnestness with which he prays against expected suffering, with the languor and unconcern of his thanksgiving afterwards, and he will soon see how little he has of the real habit of prayer, and how much his religion depends on accidental excitement, which is no test of a religious heart.

JOHN HENRY NEWMAN [118]

ROGATION MASS

Your heavenly Father will give the good spirit to those who ask it of him. (Gospel)

No one should underestimate the power of prayer since He to whom we pray did not underestimate it. He will give us either what we ask or what He knows will be more useful to us. The Lord frequently admonished his disciples to pray, often approved it by His actions, and proposed it to them by many examples in order to convince us of the power of prayer. It has indeed an unspeakable power capable of obtaining all good things and repelling all evil ones.

If therefore you want to bear adversity patiently, —pray!

If you want to trample under foot evil affections, —pray!

If you want to recognize the cunning of Satan and avoid his snares, —pray!

If you want to live joyously in the service of God and not to give way under work and affliction, —pray!

If you want to train yourself in the spiritual life and not to be preoccupied by carnal desires, —pray!

If you want to nourish your soul with good and holy thoughts and fervent and devout desires, —pray!

If you want to establish your heart manfully and firmly in the good pleasure of God, —pray!

If you want to root up vices and implant virtues, —pray!

If you want to attain to contemplation and the enjoyment of the embraces of the spouse, —pray!

If you want to taste the sweetness of heaven and the grandeurs of God, —pray!

In brief, prayer is useful in every necessity, putting demons to flight and summoning angels.

LUDOLPH THE CARTHUSIAN [119]

While God is most lavishly generous—readier to give than we are to receive—yet He wills our prayers as so many occasions for bestowing upon us the Holy Spirit's gifts of grace. He wills not only mental prayer, which is "an ascent of the mind toward God," but also oral prayer, which is "an entreaty to God for what is suitable." He wills not only personal prayer, but also prayer through the saints as through divinely appointed assistants, in order that we may gain through their intercession what our own merit has not deserved. And lest we wander astray in our uncertainty, not knowing what to ask or what is good for us, God gave us a formal prayer composed by Him, in which are contained, under seven requests, all of the things that should be sought.

This should be understood as follows. As the first Principle is supremely true and good in Himself, so also He is supremely just and merciful in His work. And because He is supremely merciful, He reaches down most lovingly to the misery of man through an infusion of His grace. However, being also supremely just, He bestows the perfect gift only upon the man who desires it. He gives grace only to the grateful, and mercy only to the one who knows his own wretchedness. Thus, freedom of the will is left unhampered, appreciation of the gift undiminished, and respect for divine honor unimpaired. Because, therefore, prayer consists in seeking divine help, adducing one's own incapacity, and giving thanks for a gratuitous favor: therefore prayer prepares for the reception of the divine gifts, and God wills to be prayed to, in order that He may lavish His bounties.

Further, if our desire is to rise aloft effectively in its quest for the divine gifts, our love must be warm, our thoughts collected, and our hope sure and strong. And because our heart is often lukewarm, distracted, and fearful by reason of a guilty conscience which makes it afraid to appear of itself before the divine countenance: therefore God willed that we pray not only MENTALLY but also ORALLY, so that the words may arouse our heart and their meaning help us gather our scattered thoughts.

He willed also that we pray through the saints, and that the saints pray for us. This was to give confidence to the fearful, so that those who dare not or cannot ask by themselves may succeed through able intercessors. Hence, in those who prayed, humility would be preserved; in the interceding saints, dignity would be manifested; and in all the members of Christ, that love and unity would be displayed by which the lower have faithful recourse to the higher while the higher generously condescend to the lower.

Finally, the just and merciful God must heed our petitions in those matters only which concern His glory and our salvation; and such are reward in the fatherland and provision along the way. Since there are three of the former and four of the latter, the petitions of the Lord's Prayer teaching us what to ask are seven in number.

ST. BONAVENTURE [120]

The Christian is bound to perform many good works, but before all else what he ought to do is to pray, for without prayer no other good work whatever can be accomplished. Without prayer he cannot find the way to the Lord, he cannot understand the truth, he cannot crucify the flesh with its passions and lusts, his heart cannot be enlightened with the light of Christ, he cannot be savingly united to God. None of those things can be effected unless they are preceded by constant prayer. I say "constant," for the perfection of prayer does not lie within our power; as the Apostle Paul says, *For we know not what we should pray for as we ought.* [Rom. 8, 26] Consequently it is just to pray often, to pray always, which falls within our power as the means of attaining purity of prayer, which is the mother of all spiritual blessings. "Capture the Mother, and she will bring you the children," said St. Isaac the Syrian. Learn first to acquire the power of prayer and you will easily practise all other virtues.

THE WAY OF A PILGRIM [121]

Ascension Time

Fifty days after the Passover the Temple at Jerusalem was the scene of a harvest festival.[1] This Thanksgiving Day had also become a solemn liturgical feast commemorating one of the greatest events in Israel's history. After the exodus from Egypt Yahweh manifested Himself to the Israelites at Sinai. Clouds, thunder, and lightning accompanied God's descent as He came down with fire about Him *so that smoke went up as if from a furnace.*[2] Loud rang the trumpet blast as the great mountain trembled in the presence of the Lord. It was in the midst of this majestic and awesome theophany that God transmitted His law to Moses and to the people. On the summit of Sinai He renewed and rendered more precise the previous covenants with Noah and Abraham.[3]

On the first Christian Pentecost, within a framework which recalled the theophanies of the Old Testament, the Holy Spirit descended upon the apostles under the appearance of tongues of fire.[4] This was no mere transmission of a covenant pact between God and men, but a gift of God's very love, of the Third Person of the Holy Trinity.[5] As at the beginning of the world when the spirit of God brooded over the waters,[6] the Spirit comes for the creation of the Church. His first act is to accord the apostles[7]

[1] Lev. 23, 15-22.
[2] Ex. 19, 18.
[3] Gen. 9, 8-17; 15, 1-21.
[4] Epistle of Pentecost, Acts 2, 3.
[5] Gospel of Pentecost, Jn. 14, 23-31.
[6] Gen. 1, 2; Offertory of the Vigil of Pentecost, Ps. 103, 30.
[7] Acts 2, 4.

that gift of tongues which immediately recalls for us the Tower of Babel.[8] Human pride, a collective pride, had been punished by a babel of languages and the consequent dispersion of men to the four quarters of the world.

Now men baptized with the Holy Spirit and with fire[9] speak in many languages and gather a great crowd bewildered and amazed at God's marvelous works. No longer is it a question of giving thanks for an abundant harvest but for an even more abundant life which is poured forth in the Church and through her to all mankind.[10] Now we rejoice in the gift of the Spirit rather than in the gift of the Law. Christians become temples of the Spirit, and the law is no longer one written in ink or carved in tablets of stone but one inscribed on human hearts by the Spirit of the living God.[11]

Such is God's great work which the Church invites us to relive and admire. It is on this day that the Church was born as the full accomplishment of the Mystery of Christ. After the Spirit of Jesus descends upon her, she becomes henceforth the sanctifying presence of God in the world. The Acts of the Apostles present this breakthrough as the coming of a great wind unloosed upon the first disciples and later upon the Gentile converts.[12] The Spirit blows where He will,[13] a kindling and luminous flame designed to set the whole world on fire. Can we bear this consuming fire? Each Pentecost should be for us that baptism with fire spoken of by John the Baptist, a baptism which purifies and transforms us,[14] unless we want it to become the fire of judgment.[15]

The charity which the Spirit confers is like refreshing morning dew, soaking into the hearts of those who are open to its influences.[16] Only the egotistical can oppose an effective barrier to

[8] Gen. 11, 1-9.

[9] As predicted by the Baptist, Mt. 3, 11.

[10] Gospel of Pentecost Tuesday, Jn. 10, 1-10.

[11] 2 Cor. 3, 3.

[12] See Epistles of this week.

[13] Communion verse of Pentecost Saturday, Jn. 3, 8.

[14] Prayer over the Offering, Vigil Mass; Collect, Pentecost Tuesday.

[15] Epistle, Ember Wednesday, Acts 2, 14. 21; First Lesson, Ember Saturday, Joel 2, 28-32.

[16] Introit and Epistle of Ember Saturday, Rom. 5, 5.

its sweet and penetrating influences. Peace and unity are the chief fruits of this charity given by the Spirit,[17] a charity whose action is ceaselessly at work in history.[18] Ever and again Christians of spiritual discernment can contemplate it in the marvels accomplished in the hearts of those whom we know and love. We can see it working from age to age in the Church as it zealously guards the precious deposit of faith; we can see it fructifying in the works of mercy all down the Church's history. Surely the moving source of all these admirable aspects of the Church is the active presence of the Spirit of love. It is this very presence which constitutes the Christian community, gives it a concrete unity, and causes it to bear fruit abundantly. Like the apostles should we not rejoice in God's marvels[19] and, God willing, contribute by witness and work to the enrichment of the Church's life and the accomplishment of new deeds which the Spirit may want to realize in us and through us? The Gospel readings for this week which recall first of all the great realities of the Church's existence—faith,[20] unity,[21] the Eucharist[22]—subsequently insist upon the miracles worked by Christ.[23] Perhaps the Church means to suggest that now God's almighty power rests within her hands. In her and through her the activity of the Holy Spirit, the inexhaustible source of holiness, touches us and transforms us as it has touched and transformed the men of all ages since the first Christian Pentecost.

THE ASCENSION OF THE LORD

HYMN FOR THE ASCENSION
The new and mystic Bread
today

[17] Collects of Monday and Friday; Communion of Wednesday, Jn. 14, 27.

[18] Introit of Pentecost, Wis. 1, 7.

[19] Acts 2, 11.

[20] Monday, Jn. 3, 16-21.

[21] Tuesday, Jn. 10, 1-10.

[22] Wednesday, Jn. 6, 44-52.

[23] From Thursday on; see also the Epistles of Wednesday and Thursday where the power of God operated through Peter and Philip.

had gone up to heaven.
What was hidden
was revealed in this body of yours
which has gone up
like an oblation.
Blessed, Lord, be your bread.

The Lamb of the house of David
came to us,
the Priest of Abraham's stock.
He came to be our Priest,
and his body is the victim
and his blood the libation.
Blessed be his sacrifice.

From heaven he came as light comes,
from Mary as a shoot from the root;
from the cross he was picked like a fruit;
he went up to heaven as our first-fruit.
Blessed be his will. . . .

You are heaven's offering and earth's:
the one slew you,
the other adored you.
You came down on earth
and there you were the Victim,
you went up to heaven
as the great Oblation.
Up you went to heaven, Lord,
bearing the offering.

ST. EPHRAEM THE SYRIAN [122]

When My only-begotten Son returned to Me, forty days after
the resurrection, this Bridge, namely Himself, arose from the
earth, that is, from among the conversation of men, and ascended
into Heaven by virtue of the Divine Nature and sat at the right
hand of Me, the Eternal Father, as the angels said, on the day of
the Ascension, to the disciples, standing like dead men, their
hearts lifted on high, and ascended into Heaven with the wisdom

of My Son—'Do not stand here any longer, for He is seated at the right hand of the Father!' When He, then, had thus ascended on high, and returned to Me the Father, I sent the Master, that is the Holy Spirit, who came to you with My power and the wisdom of My Son, and with His own clemency, which is the essence of the Holy Spirit. He is one thing with Me, the Father, and with My Son. And He built up the road of the doctrine which My Truth had left in the world. Thus, though the bodily presence of My Son left you, His doctrine remained, and the virtue of the stones founded upon this doctrine, which is the way made for you by this Bridge. For first, He practised this doctrine and made the road by His actions, giving you His doctrine by example rather than by words; for He practised, first Himself, what He afterwards taught you, then the clemency of the Holy Spirit made you certain of the doctrine, fortifying the minds of the disciples to confess the truth, and to announce this road, that is, the doctrine of Christ crucified, reproving, by this means, the world of its injustice and false judgment. . . .

Wherefore, first I gave you the Bridge of My Son living and conversing in very deed amongst men, and when He, the living Bridge, left you, there remained the Bridge and the road of His doctrine, as has been said, His doctrine being joined with My power and with His wisdom, and with the clemency of the Holy Spirit. This power of Mine gives the virtue of fortitude to whoever follows this road, wisdom gives him light, so that, in this road, he may recognize the truth, and the Holy Spirit gives him love, which consumes and takes away all sensitive love out of the soul, leaving there only the love of virtue. Thus, in both ways, both actually and through His doctrine, He is the Way, the Truth, and the Life; that is, the Bridge which leads you to the height of Heaven.

ST. CATHERINE OF SIENA [123]

SUNDAY AFTER THE ASCENSION OF THE LORD

Have a constant mutual love among yourselves. (Epistle)

Our Lord hoped for everything from everyone. From a sinner he expected purity. He loved Mary Magdalen and defended her against all the others. He defended her against Judas who accused her of waste, against Martha who accused her of idleness, and against Simon the Pharisee who treated her like a courtesan. He saw in her all the harm that people had done to her by not loving her enough, and He knew how He was going to save her from that. All those who love you have given you the means of growing spiritually just because they have loved you; they have brought out in you the being that you would never have dared to become alone, that you would never have let yourself be. We become very humble when we are really loved by someone. If anyone loves us, we very soon start saying to him, "I don't deserve it . . . you don't know what I am like . . ." It is only towards those who love us that we dare to show ourselves humble, kind, affectionate, simple, and vulnerable.

LOUIS EVELY [124]

The time is coming when whoever kills you will think he is doing service to God. (Gospel)

They have put fetters on your feet, and have bound your blessed limbs, and the temples of God with disgraceful chains, as if the spirit also could be bound with the body, or your gold could be stained by the contact of iron. To men who are dedicated to God, and attesting their faith with religious courage, such things are ornaments, not chains; nor do they bind the feet of the Christians for infamy, but glorify them for a crown. Oh feet blessedly bound, which are loosed, not by the smith but by the Lord! Oh feet blessedly bound, which are guided to paradise in the way of salvation! Oh feet bound for the present time in the world, that they may be always free with the Lord! Oh feet, lingering for a while among the fetters and cross-bars, but to run quickly to Christ on a glorious road! Let cruelty, either envious or malignant, hold you here in its bonds and chains as long as it will, from this earth and from these sufferings you shall speedily come to the kingdom of heaven. The body is not cherished in the mines with couch and cushions, but it is cherished with the refreshment and solace of Christ. The frame wearied with labours lies prostrate on the ground, but it is no penalty to lie down with Christ. Your limbs unbathed, are foul and disfigured with filth and dirt; but within they are spiritually cleansed, although without the flesh is defiled. There the bread is scarce; but man lives not by bread alone, but by the word of God. Shivering, you want clothing; but he who puts on Christ is both abundantly clothed and adorned. The hair of your half-shorn head seems repulsive; but since Christ is the head of the man, anything whatever must needs become that head which is illustrious on account of Christ's name. All that deformity, detestable and foul to Gentiles, with what splendour shall it be recompensed! This temporal and brief suffering, how shall it be exchanged for the reward of a bright and eternal honour, when, according to the word of the blessed apostle, *the Lord shall change the body of our humiliation, that it may be fashioned like to the body of His brightness*. [Phil. 3, 21]

ST. CYPRIAN [125]

SATURDAY, VIGIL OF PENTECOST

I will send you another Paraclete. (Gospel)

The word *paracletos* means first of all a legal assistant, an advocate, a defending counsel; but it also means one who speaks out prophetically, proclaiming, exhorting, enlightening; and this leads to a third meaning, one who consoles, when the message proclaimed is the message of salvation, of hope and of joy. In the first epistle of St. John [2, 1] our Lord is referred to as a paraclete or advocate who will plead our cause; and this is implicitly affirmed by Christ himself when he tells the disciples he

141

will send them another paraclete to befriend and defend them. But there is an essential difference between the mode of activity of the Spirit and that of the incarnate Word: the mission of the Spirit is the direct result of the mission of the Son: the lifting up of the Son in death and glory brings about the coming down of the pentecostal wind and fire (and thus the essential pattern of sacrifice is fulfilled; for sacrifice, like morality, is *dialogal* in structure); but the Spirit does not simply continue the work of the Son; his activity is of a different kind precisely because it is the activity of spirit whereas the work of the Son was carried out through his human flesh. So our Lord taught the multitudes, but it was as one man teaching another, through the medium of human speech which is addressed to the ear and thence the brain but may fail to penetrate the depths of the personality, to reach the heart. The Spirit will not teach men what they have never been taught before: he will teach them what they have been taught before but have failed to assimilate so fully as to be possessed by the truth in mind and heart alike. It is the hearts of men that the Spirit instructs; and instructs not by an external voice but by his indwelling presence, by being for them precisely the breath of life.

This knowledge, then, is love-knowledge: not a cold, academic apprehension of truths but an assimilation, an affinity, a living and loving union with the truth who is also goodness and beauty and light and life and love; it is the *initia* of the life which is eternal and at the same time the transfiguring process through which man is refashioned in the likeness of Love and thereby attains the joy and the peace of which our Lord now speaks: his joy, which will fill their hearts brimful; his peace, which will keep them always in good heart.

GERALD VANN [126]

Great indeed is the Holy Spirit, and in his gifts, omnipotent and wonderful. Think how, whatever number there is of you sitting here now, there is present that number of souls. On each one, he is at work to good purpose, and, as present in the midst, he sees how each is disposed. He sees alike the thoughts and consciences of each. He knows what we say and what we think and what we believe. What I have said might seem enough for us, but yet it falls short of the whole. For, with your minds enlightened by the Holy Spirit, I beg you to note how many Christians there are in the whole of the diocese, and then how many in the whole province of Palestine. Next stretch your thoughts beyond the province to take in the whole Roman empire. Then, if you please, beyond that, into the whole wide world, the people of the Persians, the nations of India, the Goths and Sarmatians, Gauls and Spaniards, Moors, Libyans, Ethiopians, and then all those others for whom we have no recognized names: for not even the appellation of many nations has ever reached us. And then think how that in each of these nations there are bishops, presbyters, deacons, religious men and women and all the other lay people. Finally contemplate the great Guardian and Dispenser of their several graces, who, throughout the world, is giving to this one chastity, and to that one lifelong virginity, making another a generous giver, and detaching another from care for worldly goods, while on yet another he bestows the gift of driving out evil spirits. And just as daylight, by one act of the sun's radiation, enlightens the whole earth, so too the Holy Spirit is giving light, to all who have eyes to see. For if anyone is unreceptive of such grace because of spiritual blindness, let him lay the blame on his own faithlessness, and not on the Spirit.

ST. CYRIL OF JERUSALEM [127]

PENTECOST SUNDAY

Suddenly there came a sound from heaven as of a violent wind coming . . . and there appeared to them parted tongues as of fire. (Lesson)

We know what a "pentecostal community" is from the account in the Acts. (1, 12; 2, 1–3) After the Lord's ascension, the eleven apostles with Mary, the mother of Jesus, and his brethren and the holy women who had attended on him, gathered together in an upper room of a house in Jerusalem, *a company of about a hundred and twenty.* [Acts 1, 15]. Ten days later, at about nine o'clock in the morning, a sound like that of a strong wind blowing filled the house, and what seemed to be tongues of fire came down *on each one of them, and they were all filled with the Holy Spirit and began to speak in strange tongues, as the Spirit gave utterance to each.* [Acts 2, 3–4]

There are several points to be noticed in this account. First, the *Pneuma* is given not merely to the apostles, but to all the hundred and twenty. The primary purpose of the sending of the *Pneuma* is therefore not the sanctification of the individual, but the uniting together of all in the one *Pneuma,* that is, the formation of the community in and through the *Pneuma.* Then, the *speaking in strange tongues* is not the sudden acquisition of linguistic talent, nor does it imply the use of any ordinary foreign tongue. It is a language which the *Pneuma* teaches them to speak, an ecstatic speech in which the hundred and twenty express to each other their jubilation in their experience of the *Pneuma.* This ecstatic experience is so overwhelming that a rational language with the natural words and constructions of earthly speech is powerless to express it. It is a speech of heavenly origin, or, as Bousset says, "the language of angels for revealing the mysteries of a heavenly world." The mystery which the hundred and twenty experienced within themselves was none other than the mystery of the Church, *which is his [Christ's] Body, the fullness of him who fills all in all.* [Eph. 1, 23] Thus, through the sending of the *Pneuma,* Whitsun is indeed the birthday of the Church, which now manifests itself for the first time in this company of a hundred and twenty as a community in the Spirit, a "pneumatic" Church.

JOHANNES PINSK [128]

Mary, spiritual mother of the Christian community.

The disciple whom Jesus loved can say of Mary that she is the Mother of Jesus and also his own mother; he realizes then the intimacy which unites him with Christ, his Lord and his brother. Mary, the Mother of Jesus and his mother, is the person who is able to draw him closer to Christ, his Lord and his God. With him, she has been a witness of the last moments of the Crucifixion, she has heard the last words of Jesus, and has received the Spirit which He has transmitted to the Church. Mary is therefore for him, and, through him, for all the disciples, and for the Church which gathers about them, a very close sign of the presence of the Lord, a spiritual mother in the Christian community, the most venerated of all spiritual mothers found in the Church, the spiritual mother par excellence of the beloved and faithful disciple, of the brother of Jesus, which every Christian is called to be.

Immediately after the Ascension, we see, in the Acts of the Apostles [1, 12–14], the group of the Eleven, returning to Jerusalem and going into the Upper Room where they had habitually met with Christ. There they are to await the outpouring of the Spirit at Pentecost. *All these with one accord devoted themselves to prayer, together with the women, Mary, the mother of Jesus, and with his brothers.* [Acts 1, 14] Mary, the Mother of Jesus, is here integrated with the whole group of the disciples: the apostles, the women and the relatives of the Lord. With them, and in the midst of them, being of one heart and mind with them, she is assiduous in prayer, awaiting the great outpouring of the Holy Spirit which will open the missionary era of the Church. A type of Mother Church, she has no place of a ministerial or hierarchical kind, as have Peter, John, James and the other Apostles who are first named. She is mentioned among the women and relatives of Jesus. She is in the midst of the primitive Church, as a humble and praying example, as a handmaid of the Lord and of the Church. It is thus that she will receive the Spirit at Pentecost, in order that she may be fulfilled with the fullness of her vocation, in the very heart of the Church.

She appears indeed as the widow of the ancient Church *who sets her hope on God and continues in supplication and prayer night and day.* [1 Tim. 5, 5] However, she is not alone; she has a son in the disciple whom Jesus loved; she is the spiritual mother par excellence in the midst of the faithful women who have followed Christ and who are always there. She is for the disciple, and for all the disciples, the type of Mother Church and the spiritual mother rediscovered in the Church. In the power of the Spirit, she will be able to transmit to the disciples and to the primitive Church all that she knew of Jesus, her beloved Son, and what she has so preciously guarded and pondered in her

145

heart. [Lk. 2, 19, 51] She will be a humble bearer of the Gospel of her Son, not in the same fashion as the missionary apostles, but in the manner of a discreet and loving mother, a human mother, the mother of the Son of God whom she has known better than any one in the intimacy of His company, a spiritual mother of the disciples, to recall all that Christ said and did, and of whom she has been able to be a faithful and attentive hearer. By her faith, her hope, her charity, and her prayers she will be a spiritual mother of Mother Church, of whom she is the living and humble representative.

MAX THURIAN [129]

GOD'S GRANDEUR

The world is charged with the grandeur of God.
   It will flame out, like shining from shook foil;
   It gathers to a greatness, like the ooze of oil
Crushed. Why do men then now not reck his rod?
Generations have trod, have trod, have trod;
   And all is seared with trade; bleared, smeared with toil;
   And wears man's smudge and shares man's smell: the soil
Is bare now, nor can foot feel, being shod.

And for all this, nature is never spent;
   There lives the dearest freshness deep down things;
And though the last lights off the black West went
   Oh, morning, at the brown bring eastward, springs—
Because the Holy Ghost over the bent
   World broods with warm breast and with ah! bright wings.

GERARD MANLEY HOPKINS [130]

Lord, give us your Spirit. Grant us the fruits of the Spirit which according to the apostle are: *charity, joy, peace, patience, benignity, goodness, faith mildness, modesty, continence.* [Gal. 5, 22] If we have the Spirit and his fruits, then we are no longer slaves of the law but free children of God. The Spirit cries out in us: Abba, Father. He intercedes for us with unspeakable groanings. He is the anointing, the seal and surety of eternal life. He is the fount of eternal water which has its source in the heart

146

and rises up to eternal life, whispering: Come! Come home to the Father!

Jesus, send us the Spirit. Give us again and again your Pentecostal gift. Make our spiritual eye bright and our spiritual awareness sensitive, so that we are able to distinguish your Spirit from all others. Give us your Spirit, that it may be said of us: *And if the Spirit of him who raised up Jesus from the dead dwell in you; he that raised up Jesus Christ from the dead shall quicken also your mortal bodies, because of his Spirit that dwells in you.* [Rom. 8, 11]

Lord, may Pentecost be ever with us. Your servants and handmaids ask with the boldness which you require of them: May Pentecost be in us also. Now and for ever. Amen.

KARL RAHNER [131]

The Holy Spirit, God's Gift.

Each of the three Divine Persons is holy, and each is a spirit, and we give the name "Holy Spirit" to the Third Person precisely because He is all that the Father and Son have in common—their divinity, their charity, their blessedness, their delight in each other, their holiness, and their spiritual nature. The Son comes from the Father by generation, and the Holy Spirit comes from the Father and the Son in virtue of a procession which is proper to Him. But He comes principally from the Father, since it is from the Father (and not from Himself) that the Son has the power to be a co-principle of the procession of the Holy Spirit. In virtue of His generation by the Father, the Son Who is God of God is one with God the Father. But although it is equally true that the Father and the Holy Spirit are One, it does not follow (indeed it were false to claim) that the Son receives His being from the Holy Spirit as well as from the Father.

The Holy Spirit is the Spirit of the Father and the Son, proceeding from them both, and He is the unity and charity of them both. It is clear that He is not a mere link between Father and Son, by means of which the Son is loved by His Father and the Father by His only begotten Son. This would make them distinct only by their participation in the Divine essence, and not

147

in virtue of the essence itself. It would make them one by reason of another's gift, and not by their own unity of spirit. That the Holy Spirit is co-essential with the Father and the Son, is implied by the very fact that He proceeds from them Both. But in that He is sent to us men, He is manifested as God's gift to us. The Holy Spirit is so completely, so truly, God's gift, that unless a man has the Holy Spirit, he has none of God's gift, and whoever has any of them, has them only in the Holy Spirit. Many things are given to us through the Holy Spirit, but they are valueless if the chief gift of charity is lacking. And the reason why the Holy Spirit is called 'Gift of God' is because *the charity of God is poured forth in our hearts, by the Holy Ghost Who is given to us.* [Rom. 5, 5]

Nothing is more excellent than this gift, which ultimately differentiates between the sons of the kingdom and the children of darkness. Even if all the other gifts are lacking, charity will take us to the kingdom of God. Although faith can exist without charity, only the faith that works through love can have any value. The Holy Spirit is the charity of the Father and the Son, by means of which they love each other. He is the unity in virtue of which they are one. When He is given to men, He enkindles in their hearts the love of God and of their fellow men. This same love, living in men's hearts, is the love by which God is love. . . . This is *the spirit of the Lord* [*that*] *fills the whole world.* [Wis. 1, 7] with His all-powerful goodness, appointing a perfect harmony among all creatures, and filling them all with the vast riches of His grace, according to the capacity of each. . . . It is He Who teaches us to pray as we ought, making us cleave to God, rendering us pleasing to God and not unworthy to have our prayers answered. He enlightens our minds, and forms love in our hearts. All this is the work of the Holy Spirit. We may even call it His own special work, if we remember that He is sufficient for this task only because He can never be separated from the Father and the Son. Whatever action the Holy Spirit performs, is done in concert with the Father and the Son from Whom He is inseparable.

WILLIAM OF ST. THIERRY [132]

148

MONDAY WITHIN THE OCTAVE OF PENTECOST

The Holy Spirit descended on all who heard the message. (Epistle)

The Church is the body of Christ through its union with the Saviour in his death and resurrection. Having become the body of Christ in his death and resurrection, the Church dies to the flesh with the Saviour and rises again in the Spirit through the unique vivifying action of the Father, the action which vivifies Christ. Thus the outpouring of the Spirit is one in the Church, although its manifestations are varied to infinity, for it is no other than the action of the Father raising up Christ, unique in itself and from which all the faithful draw life. The outpouring of the Spirit has for its object, by an equal title, both the body of Christ and the faithful who are the body of Christ. The gift of the Spirit who raises up the faithful is not distinct from the Spirit which raised up the Saviour, since the faithful find their justification, progressive sanctification, and final resurrection in their participation in the resurrection of Christ. There is but one outpouring of the Spirit, the one that glorifies Christ.

F. X. DURRWELL [133]

The Holy Spirit, the Comforter.

To comfort you must love. You must be open and enter into the other's heart. You must be observant; you must have the free and sensitive heart which finds the paths of life with quiet assurance; you must be able to discover the sore and withered places. You must have subtlety and strength to penetrate to the living center, to the deep source of life which has dried up. The heart must combine with this source of life, must summon it to life again so that it can flow through all the deserts and ruins within. To do this is truly to comfort. To do this is to awaken, to generate, to create. To do this is to call forth the best in the other person. Such comfort liberates in the very act of permeat-

149

ing. It releases, supports, and broadens, but in such a way that the other rises again from his own true center and makes a fresh beginning.

A person who has been wounded is comforted when someone who loves him awakens the hidden energy within him so that it passes through the wound in a healing stream . . . a person who is spiritually dried up is comforted when someone who loves him releases the wave of life within and everything is revived . . . a person who has lost things of great value, who had had his work destroyed and his hopes dashed, is comforted when someone who loves him allies himself with something that lies at a deeper level, underneath the individual possession and the individual work, allies himself with the fundamental creative will, and rouses it to new activity, allies himself with that innermost soul that is above all change and loss and is the eternal strength of the heart; admitting the loss that is lost in time, but winning it anew from the timelessness of faith in God; a person whose heart is sullied is comforted when someone who loves him is able to touch the purity which lives below the sin, and rouse a new confidence in his ability to overcome the ugliness of his heart; a person who has sinned and can find no escape from his troubled conscience is comforted when someone who loves him is able, without the slightest presumption, to shed light on the sinner's self-deception, to release and fortify the will and open up new ways and possibilities. There is comfort when the lover is able to soften the hardened, to touch the paralyzed with relaxing warmth, to give a new direction to an erring mind.

Human love, really pure and selfless human love, is able to comfort. But it soon attains its limits. Human love is not the love of God.

Christ sent us the One who is "the nearness" between the Father and the Son: the Holy Spirit. He is the only inwardness of God Himself; in the secret language of love He is the "tie," the "kiss." In Him God has come to us as the Comforter.

ROMANO GUARDINI [134]

Come, Holy Spirit, fill the hearts of your faithful, and kindle in them the fire of your love. (Alleluia verse)

Then we realise that the whole universe is a sacrament, which mirrors the divine reality; that each created thing, though nothing in itself, is of infinite value and significance because it is the sign of a mystery, which is enshrined in the depths of its being. Then every human being is known to be not merely an isolated individual carried along on the flux of time and doomed to extinction, but a member of a divine society, working out its destiny in space and time and subject to all the tragic consequences of subservience to the material world, but destined to transcend the limitations of time and space and mortality and to enter into that fullness of life where there shall be *neither mourning nor weeping nor pain any more.* [Ap. 21, 4] The suffering of this world can have no meaning as long as we attempt to judge it in the light of this present time. We are like people who hear snatches of music, which they have no means of relating to the symphony as a whole. But when we have passed beyond the conditions of this present life we shall then have that integral knowledge in which the whole is known in every part and every part is seen to mirror the whole.

This is a certainty which only faith can give, but even now we can begin to discern something of the truth. For love can give us a kind of knowledge which is beyond both faith and reason. The divine mystery is ultimately a mystery of love, and it reveals itself to love alone. It is only if we are prepared to give ourselves totally in love that Love will give itself totally to us. Then we shall discover that the power which "moves the sun and the other stars" is indeed a power of love; that it is this that lies at the heart of our human existence and shapes our lives. But it is a love which revealed itself in an agony of self-surrender on the Cross, and only makes itself known to those who are prepared to make the same surrender. For the love of God is not a mild benevolence; it is a consuming fire. To those who resist it it becomes an eternal torment; to those who are willing to face its demands, it becomes a fire that cleanses and purifies; those whom it has once penetrated, it transforms into itself. . . .

If we are ever to find peace either in ourselves or in the world we shall have to learn again that ancient wisdom which alone can give man peace with nature and with God, and which was summed up by Dostoevsky in the words of the Prior of the monastery in which the Brothers Karamazov met: "Brothers, have no fear of men's sin. Love a man even in his sin, for that is the semblance of divine love, and is the highest love on earth. Love all God's creation, the whole and every grain of sand in it. Love every leaf and every ray of God's light. Love the animals, love the plants, love everything. If you love everything you will perceive the divine mystery in things. Once you perceive it, you will begin to comprehend it better every day. And you will come at last to love the whole world with an all-embracing love."

BEDE GRIFFITHS [135]

EMBER WEDNESDAY AFTER PENTECOST

The bread which I shall give is my flesh for the life of the world.
(Gospel)

The Eucharist is the sacrament of the redemptive mystery of the cross which it symbolizes, celebrates and makes present. It is, in addition, the sacrament of the unity of the Mystical Body, which it is its special grace to bring into being. . . .

In the Eucharist we receive Christ in the form of food. In consequence, according to the law of the sacraments, whose special effects result from what they signify, we unite ourselves to Christ in a mysterious union similar to that obtaining between a living being and its food. In the natural order, the living thing assimilates its food and incorporates it into its own substance. Here, however, the roles are reversed but the effect is mysteriously alike. The Eucharist is food and it is certainly our own soul that it feeds with that incorruptible food which is Christ. But whereas, in the natural and material order, all the power of assimilation resides in us so that we reduce what we eat to form part of our own life, here the power of assimilation belongs to Christ and it is he who, in feeding us, unites us and incorporates us with his life. What Truth said to St. Augustine may be applied to the Eucharist: " 'Eat me and grow in stature. But it is not you who will change me into yourself, like bodily food, it is I who will change you into me.' " (*Confessions*, VII, 10)

The union with Christ which results, an infinitely mysterious one, is like the union which takes place in a living thing; it is both an incorporation and an intensification of life. For, as we have seen, Our Lord compares in the most explicit fashion the union he wishes to establish between us and himself, especially through the Eucharist, to the unity existing between him and his Father, and that is a unity of perfect life, a substantial unity of life . . .

The Eucharist is, then, the perfect sacrament of our incorporation with Christ. Theologians are unanimous in holding that its special effect is to bring about the unity of the Mystical Body. By a special increase of grace and of living faith, it incorporates us with Christ precisely inasmuch as it takes us all into the supreme act of love by which he offered himself for us on the cross, *so as to bring together into one all God's children, scattered far and wide*. [Jn. 11, 52]

We cannot, then, communicate in isolation from our brethren. We communicate in the true body of Christ only by communicating at the same time in his Mystical Body; the "breaking of bread" brings with it, inseparably, the presence of Christ uniting us to himself and that of the multitude which shares in his redemption—*the one bread makes us one body, though we are many in number*. [1 Cor. 10, 17] There we have the whole mystery of the Mystical Body.

YVES CONGAR [136]

I am the bread of life. (Gospel)

Holy Scripture is the table of Christ,
from whence we are nourished,
from whence we learn what we should love

153

and what we should desire,
to whom
we should have our eyes raised.

ALCUIN 137

THURSDAY WITHIN THE OCTAVE OF PENTECOST

Jesus sent them out to proclaim the kingdom of God. (Gospel)

Christians are not distinguished from the rest of mankind by either country, speech, or customs; the fact is, they nowhere settle in cities of their own; they use no peculiar language; they cultivate no eccentric mode of life. Certainly, this creed of theirs is no discovery due to some fancy or speculation of inquisitive men; nor do they, as some do, champion a doctrine of human origin. Yet while they dwell in both Greek and non-Greek cities, as each one's lot was cast, and conform to the customs of the country in dress, food, and mode of life in general, the whole tenor of their way of living stamps it as worthy of admiration and admittedly extraordinary. They reside in their respective countries, but only as aliens. They take part in everything as citizens and put up with everything as foreigners. Every foreign land is their home, and every home a foreign land. They marry like all others and beget chidren; but they do not expose their offspring. Their board they spread for all, but not their bed. They find themselves *in the flesh,* but do not live *according to the flesh.* They spend their days on earth, but hold citizenship in heaven. They obey the established laws, but in their private lives they rise above the laws. They love all men, but are persecuted by all. They are unknown, yet are condemned; they are put to death, but it is life that they receive. *They are poor, and enrich many* [2 Cor. 6, 10]; destitute of everything, they abound in everything. They are dishonored, and in their dishonor find their glory. They are calumniated, and are vindicated. *They are reviled, and they bless* [1 Cor. 4, 12]; they are insulted and render honor. Doing good, they are penalized as evildoers; when penalized, they rejoice because they are quickened into life. The Jews make war

154

on them as foreigners; the Greeks persecute them; and those who hate them are at a loss to explain their hatred.

In a word: what the soul is in the body, that the Christians are in the world. The soul is spread through all the members of the body, and the Christians throughout the cities of the world. The soul dwells in the body, but is not part and parcel of the body; so Christians dwell in the world, but are not part and parcel of the world. Itself invisible, the soul is kept shut up in the visible body; so Christians are known as such in the world, but their religion remains invisible. The flesh, though suffering no wrong from the soul, yet hates and makes war on it, because it is hindered from indulging its passions; so, too, the world, though suffering no wrong from Christians, hates them because they oppose its pleasures. The soul loves the flesh that hates it, and its members; so, too, Christians love those that hate them. The soul is locked up in the body, yet is the very thing that holds the body together; so, too, Christians are shut up in the world as in a prison, yet it is precisely they that hold the world together. Immortal, the soul is lodged in a mortal tenement; so, too, Christians, though residing as strangers among corruptible things, look forward to the incorruptibility that awaits them in heaven. The soul, when stinting itself in food and drink, fares the better for it; so, too, Christians, when penalized, show a daily increase in numbers on that account. Such is the important post to which God has assigned them, and they are not at liberty to desert it.

THE EPISTLE TO DIOGNETUS [138]

EMBER FRIDAY AFTER PENTECOST

O blessed light, fill the inmost hearts of your faithful.
(Sequence)

The secrets of Holy Scripture are locked away and sealed with the signet of God's finger, which is the Holy Spirit, so that none may learn them without His love and grace. God alone holds the key of knowledge, as Scripture says, and He Himself is the key. He admits whom He will by the inspiration of His grace, and does not break the seal. And this is how God treats those who love Him. He does not treat all in the same way, but grants special favours to those who are inspired to seek truth in the Scriptures after devout prayer and diligent study. These may learn the truths of God when He chooses to reveal them. . . .

A soul can only learn by experience what comfort and spiritual joy, savour, and sweetness this light of grace may bring to it, whether inward perceptions, hidden knowledge, and sudden visitations of the Holy Spirit. And I am sure that such a soul will not go astray provided that its teeth—that is, its spiritual senses —are kept white and clean from pride and intellectual presumption. I think that David was experiencing great joy in this way when he said: *How sweet are Your words to my lips, O Lord; sweeter than honey to my mouth.* [Ps. 118, 103] That is: O Lord God, Your holy words, recorded in Holy Scripture and brought to my mind by grace, are sweeter to my lips—that is, to the affections of my soul—than honey to my mouth. How wonderful it is to see God in this way without wearisome labour!

WALTER HILTON [139]

Who can forgive sins, but God alone? (Gospel)

The Church is built up essentially by the co-operation of the Holy Spirit sent by Christ with the apostolic ministry he established— a kind of "con-celebration" of the visible ministry with the divine Person, as is so wonderfully expressed by the Eastern Liturgy.

This is the reason why all the more important acts of the ministry so instituted, that is of the hierarchical ministry, have the divine warrant in virtue of which, for example, when a priest absolves, it is truly God who absolves; when he consecrates the bread and wine, it is truly the power of Christ and the Last Supper that acts; when two Christians marry according to the laws of the Christian community, their "I will" is written in heaven and possesses a divine sacramental value. That is why the great doctrinal decisions or simply the unanimous affirmation of the episcopal body centred on Peter have the certainty and the value of God's own witness. It is not on account of the men who are ministers of the Church, but through the Holy Ghost who is the soul of the Church and of all that, in the Church, which belongs to its essence and concerns the actual building up of the people of God.

This explains the strong terms used by the earliest Fathers, martyrs too, like St. Irenaeus and St. Hippolytus (second and early third centuries), such as "Where the Church is, there is to be found the Holy Ghost and all grace."

YVES CONGAR [140]

EMBER SATURDAY AFTER PENTECOST

I must proclaim the kingdom of God, for this is why I have been sent. (Gospel)

It is not the missioner who is missionary, it is the Church. The Church is missionary because her very nature consists in being, in this world, a foretaste of the world to come. The center of her life, which is the holy Eucharist, is a memorial of the past in view of the future, *announcing the Lord's death until he come.* But when the past and the future coincide with the present moment, we have more than past, present, or future: we have an eternal present, eternity, a participation, here on earth, in the very life of God. This relates immediately to the nature of missions. For preaching the good news of salvation makes the word of God echo in time; it brings the eternal into the texture of history. The center of all presentation of the Gospel is precisely the sacramental act by which the Church communes with her Lord. This liturgical action constitutes God's embassy to the world; it is the sacrifice in which heaven receives the first-fruits of redemption in the form of the body and blood of Christ; and it is the offering in which heaven receives the first-born from among the dead, the resurrected Christ. If the Church's mission consists in preaching the Gospel, the liturgy forms the core of this preaching. And no other preaching is legitimate unless it is related to this. Every activity, be it teaching or doing, which is an extension of this is missionary. An activity which is not an extension of this cannot be missionary.

157

In other words, the mission is not a specialized apostolate. It is not the property of missionary congregations or societies; nor is it the sum total of all missionary groups. It is not restricted to what is deliberately done for the propagation of the faith. The mission is the whole Church. The liturgical life of the whole Church has a missionary structure. She holds herself in readiness to announce the coming of the Lord. Her existence is a proclamation that the Lord is coming, that this world will pass and make way for the world of which it is but a shadow and a foretaste.

GEORGE TAVARD [141]

Sanctoral

"Lilith," said Mara, "you will not sleep, if you lie there a thousand years, until you have opened your hand and yielded that which is not yours to give or to withhold." "I cannot," she answered, "I would if I could, for I am weary, and the shadows of death are gathering about me." —"They will gather and gather, but they cannot infold you while yet your hand remains unopened. You may think you are dead, but it will only be a dream; you may think you have come awake, but it will still be only a dream. Open your hand, and you will sleep indeed—then wake indeed." —"I am trying hard, but the fingers have grown together and into the palm." —"I pray you put forth the strength of your will. For the love of life, draw together your forces and break its bonds!"

The princess turned her eyes upon Eve, beseechingly. "There was a sword I once saw in your husband's hands," she murmured. "I fled when I saw it. I heard him who bore it say it would divide whatever was not one and indivisible."

"I have the sword," said Adam. "The angel gave it me when he left the gate."

"Bring it, Adam," pleaded Lilith, "and cut me off this hand that I may sleep."

"I will," he answered.

GEORGE MACDONALD 142

March

MARCH 12
ST. GREGORY THE GREAT

Born in Rome of a noble family around 540, Gregory abandoned a political career—he was prefect of the City—disposed of his immense riches for the benefit of the poor, and founded seven monasteries. Pope Pelagius II took him from his Coelian monastery and made him papal nuncio to Constantinople (578–586). He returned to Rome in 586 and was elected pope in January of 590. He died in 604.

After St. Augustine, from whom he drew so much of his inspiration, Gregory exercised perhaps the greatest influence over the mind of the medieval Church. His justly famous Book of Pastoral Care *became not only a handbook for bishops but the very marrow of the moral and mystical ideal of medieval theology.*

The Life of the Pastor.

The conduct of a prelate should so far surpass the conduct of the people, as the life of a pastor sets him apart from his flock. For one who is so regarded that the people are called his flock, must carefully consider how necessary it is for him to maintain a life of rectitude. It is necessary, therefore, that he should be pure in thought, exemplary in conduct, discreet in keeping silence, profitable in speech, in sympathy a near neighbour to everyone, in contemplation exalted above all others, a humble companion to those who lead good lives, erect in his zeal for righteousness against the vices of sinners. He must not be remiss in his care for the inner life by preoccupation with the external; nor must he in his solicitude for what is internal, fail to give attention to the external.

ST. GREGORY [143]

The dangers of activism.

Let the ruler not relax the care of the inner life by preoccupying himself with external matters, nor should his solicitude for the inner life bring neglect of the external, lest, being engrossed with what is external, he be ruined inwardly, or being preoccupied with what concerns only his inner self, he does not bestow on his neighbours the necessary external care. For often some persons, forgetting that they are superiors of their brethren for the sake of their souls, devote themselves with all concentration of heart to secular cares. These they gladly attend to when the occasion offers, but when the occasion is not present, hanker after them day and night with the surge of a disordered mind. When they find a respite from these occupations, because the occasion for them has gone by, they are the more wearied by the respite itself. For they take it as a pleasure to be weighed down by such activities, and regard it laborious not to be labouring in earthly concerns. And so it happens that, while they rejoice in being weighed down with tumultuous worldly business, they disregard those interior matters which they ought to be teaching others. Consequently, the life of their subjects undoubtedly grows languid, because, though these wish to make spiritual progress, they are confronted with the stumbling blocks, as it were, of the example of their superior.

For when the head languishes, the members have no vigour. It is in vain that an army, seeking contact with the enemy, hurries behind its leader, if he has lost the way. No exhortation then uplifts the minds of subjects, no reproof castigates their faults, for when one who is a spiritual guardian fulfills the office of a judge of the world, the shepherd's care of the flock is lacking; and subjects cannot see the light of the truth, for when earthly cares occupy the pastor's mind, dust, driven by the winds of temptation, blinds the eyes of the Church.

ST. GREGORY [144]

164

On patience.

To preserve the virtue of patience, the sick are to be admonished ever to bear in mind how great were the evils endured constantly by our Redeemer at the hands of those whom He had created, how many horrible insults of reproaches He endured, how many blows in the face He received at the hands of scoffers, while He was daily snatching the souls of captives from the power of the ancient Enemy; that while cleansing us with the water of salvation, He did not screen His face from the spitting of perfidious men, that He silently endured the scourging to free us by His mediation from eternal torments, that He endured buffeting to give us everlasting honours among the choirs of angels, that while saving us from being pierced by our sins, He did not shrink from offering His head to thorns; that He took bitter gall in His thirst in order to inebriate us with everlasting sweetness, that when mockingly adored, He held His peace and adored in our behalf the Father, though equal to Him in the Godhead, and that He who was the life passed to death that He might prepare life for those who were dead. Why, then, is it considered hard that a man should endure stripes from God for his evil-doing, if God endured so great evil in requital for His own good deeds? Or what man is there of sane mind who is ungrateful for being himself smitten, when He who lived here without sin did not depart hence without a scourging?

ST. GREGORY 145

Preaching in word and deed.

Every preacher should make himself heard rather by deeds than by words, and that by his righteous way of life should imprint footsteps for men to tread in, rather than show them by word the way to go. For that cock, too, which the Lord in His figure of speech took as a symbol of the good preacher, when he is preparing to crow, first shakes his wings, and beating himself with them, makes himself more alert. So, it is obviously necessary that they who give utterance to words of holy preaching, should first be awake in the earnest practice of good deeds, lest, being themselves slack in performing them, they stir up others by words only. Let them first rouse themselves up by lofty deeds, and then make others solicitous to live good lives. Let them first smite themselves with the wings of their thoughts. Let them carefully examine themselves and discover in what respects they are idling and lagging, and make amends by severe penance. Then, and only then, let them set in order the lives of others by their words. They should first take heed to punish their own sins by tears, and then declare what deserves punishment in others; and before they utter words of exhortation, they should proclaim in their deeds all that they are about to say.

ST. GREGORY [146]

MARCH 17
ST. PATRICK

Patrick, the son of a British deacon, was in his youth kidnapped by Irish pirates and enslaved for many years. After his escape he determined to put his knowledge of Gaelic language and culture to good use by returning to Ireland as its apostle. He died in 461.

Patrick sang this hymn when ambuscades were laid against his coming that he might not go to Tara, the residence of the high kings of Ireland, to sow the faith.

I arise to-day
    through a mighty strength, the invocation of the Trinity,
    through belief in the Threeness,
    through confession of the Oneness
    towards the Creator.

I arise to-day
    through the strength of Christ with His Baptism,
    through the strength of His Crucifixion with His Burial,

through the strength of His Resurrection with His Ascension,
through the strength of His descent for the Judgment of Doom.

I arise to-day
    through the strength of the love of Cherubim,
    in obedience of Angels,
    in the service of the Archangels,
    in hope of resurrection to meet with reward,
    in prayers of Patriarchs,
    in predictions of Prophets,
    in preachings of Apostles,
    in faiths of Confessors,
    in innocence of Holy Virgins,
    in deeds of righteous men.

I arise to-day
    through the strength of Heaven:
    light of Sun,
    brilliance of Moon,
    splendour of Fire,
    speed of Lightning,
    swiftness of Wind,
    depth of Sea,
    stability of Earth,
    firmness of Rock.

I arise to-day
    through God's strength to pilot me:
    God's might to uphold me,
    God's wisdom to guide me,
    God's eye to look before me,
    God's ear to hear me,
    God's word to speak for me,
    God's hand to guard me,
    God's way to lie before me,
    God's shield to protect me,
    God's host to secure me—
        against snares of devils,

against temptations of vices,
against inclinations of nature,
against everyone who shall wish me ill,
   afar and anear,
alone and in a crowd. . . .
Christ to protect me to-day
   against poison, against burning,
   against drowning, against wounding,
   so that there may come abundance of reward.
Christ with me, Christ before me, Christ behind me,
Christ in me, Christ beneath me, Christ above me,
Christ on my right, Christ on my left,
Christ where I lie, Christ where I sit, Christ where I arise,
Christ in the heart of every man who thinks of me,
Christ in the mouth of every man who speaks of me,
Christ in every eye that sees me,
Christ in every ear that hears me.

I arise to-day
   through a mighty strength, the invocation of the Trinity,
   through belief in the Threeness,
   through confession of the Oneness
   towards the Creator.

Salvation is of the Lord.
Salvation is of the Lord.
Salvation is of Christ.
May Thy salvation, O Lord, be ever with us.

ST. PATRICK [147]

MARCH 21

ST. BENEDICT

This Patriarch of the Monks of the West (c. 480–555) bequeathed a Rule and a monastic way of life to the Western Church which is the fruit of years of meditation on earlier monastic experiments and the living of them as a hermit and as the father of several communities of monks. His Rule completed the break with the earlier more individualistic monasticism and or-

ganized each house of monks into a tight-knit family under a spiritual father who was the master of the "school of the Lord's service." Little by little, by reason of its balanced combination of work, study, and prayer and papal and imperial favoritism, the Benedictine Rule imposed itself upon almost all the monasteries of medieval Europe. Even today it remains one of the basic spiritual documents of the Western Church and a permanent source of inspiration for the "religious" life.

Prologue to the Holy Rule.

Listen, my son, to your master's precepts, and incline the ear of your heart. Receive willingly and carry out effectively your loving father's advice, that by the labor of obedience you may return to Him from whom you had departed by the sloth of disobedience.

To you, therefore, my words are now addressed, whoever you may be, who are renouncing your own will to do battle under the Lord Christ, the true King, and are taking up the strong, bright weapons of obedience.

And first of all, whatever good work you begin to do, beg of Him with most earnest prayer to perfect it, that He who has now deigned to count us among His sons may not at any time be grieved by our evil deeds. For we must always so serve Him with the good things He has given us, that He will never as an angry Father disinherit His children, nor ever as a dread Lord, provoked by our evil actions, deliver us to everlasting punishment as wicked servants who would not follow Him to glory. . . .

Therefore we must prepare our hearts and our bodies to do battle under the holy obedience of His commands; and let us ask God that He be pleased to give us the help of His grace for anything which our nature finds hardly possible. And if we want to escape the pains of hell and attain life everlasting, then while there is still time, while we are still in the body and are able to fulfil all these things by the light of this life, we must hasten to do now what will profit us for eternity.

And so we are going to establish a school for the service of the Lord. In founding it we hope to introduce nothing harsh or burdensome. But if a certain strictness results from the dictates of equity for the amendment of vices or the preservation of charity, do not be at once dismayed and fly from the way of salvation, whose entrance cannot but be narrow. For as we advance in the religious life and in faith, our hearts expand and we run the way of God's commandments, with unspeakable sweetness of love. Thus, never departing from His school, but persevering in the monastery according to His teaching until death, we may by patience share in the sufferings of Christ and deserve to have a share also in His kingdom.

What kind of man the abbot ought to be. (Rule, Chapter 2)

The Abbot should always remember what he is and what he is called, and should know that to whom more is committed, from him more is required. Let him understand also what a difficult and arduous task he has undertaken: ruling souls and adapting himself to a variety of characters. One he must coax, another scold, another persuade, according to each one's character and understanding. Thus he must adjust and adapt himself to all in such a way that he may not only suffer no loss in the flock committed to his care, but may even rejoice in the increase of a good flock.

Above all let him not neglect or undervalue the welfare of the souls committed to him, in a greater concern for fleeting, earthly, perishable things; but let him always bear in mind that he has undertaken the government of souls and that he will have to give an account of them.

And if he be tempted to allege a lack of earthly means, let him remember what is written: *First seek the kingdom of God and His Justice, and all these things shall be given you besides.* [Mt. 6, 33] And again, *Nothing is wanting to those who fear Him.* [Ps. 33, 10]

Let him know, then, that he who has undertaken the government of souls must prepare himself to render an account of them. Whatever number of brethren he knows he has under his care, he may be sure beyond doubt that on Judgment Day he will have to give the Lord an account of all these souls, as well as of his own soul.

Thus the constant apprehension about his coming examination as shepherd concerning the sheep entrusted to him, and his anxiety over the account that must be given for others, make him careful of his own record. And while by his admonitions he is helping others to amend, he himself is cleansed of his faults.

ST. BENEDICT [148]

MARCH 25
THE ANNUNCIATION
OF THE BLESSED VIRGIN MARY

Some ancient martyrologies gave this feast the title "the Annunciation of the Divine Incarnation to the Blessed Virgin Mary." It is a very old feast, celebrated at Constantinople already in the fifth century. It was particularly dear to English Catholics in the Middle Ages; they counted it the first day of the year.

You will conceive and bear a son and you shall give him the name Jesus . . . for nothing is impossible to God! (Gospel)

Mary and Eve.

In accordance with this design, Mary the Virgin is found obedient, saying *Behold the handmaid of the Lord, be it done unto me according to your word.* [Lk. 1, 38] But Eve was disobedient; for she did not obey when as yet she was a virgin. And even as she, having indeed a husband, Adam, but being nevertheless as yet a virgin, having become disobedient, was made the cause of death both to herself and the whole human race; so also did Mary, having a man betrothed to her and being nevertheless a virgin, by yielding obedience, became the cause of salvation, both to herself and the whole human race. And on this account does the law term a woman betrothed to a man the wife of him who had betrothed her, although she was as yet a virgin; thus indicating

171

the back reference from Mary to Eve, because what is joined together could not otherwise be put asunder than by inversion of the process by which these bonds of union had arisen, so that the former knots be cancelled by the latter, that the latter set the former again at liberty. And it has in fact happened, that the first compact looses from the second tie, but that the second tie takes the position of the first, which had been cancelled. For this reason did the Lord declare that the first should in truth be the last, and the last first. And the prophet too indicates the same, saying, *Instead of fathers, children have been born unto you.* [Ps. 44, 17] For the Lord, having been born the First-begotten of the dead and receiving into his bosom the ancient Fathers, has regenerated them unto the life of God, he having been made himself the beginning of those that live, as Adam became the beginning of those who die. Wherefore also Luke, commencing the genealogy with the Lord, carried it back to Adam, indicating that it was he who regenerated them into the gospel of life, and not they him. And thus also it was that the knot of Eve's disobedience was loosed by the obedience of Mary. For what the virgin Eve had bound fast through unbelief, this did the virgin Mary set free through faith.

ST. IRENAEUS [149]

The Annunciation begins what John later joyously proclaimed: *And the word became flesh.* (Jn. 1, 14) This is the victory of God over all Godlessness; this is the triumph of grace over all opposition; this is the unexpected and incomprehensible revelation of the immense love of God. The magnificence of the salvation-news that was brought to us by the Incarnate Son of God is already anticipated at one stroke, when Gabriel says to Mary: *You have found grace before God. You "will conceive and bear a Son." He will be great and will be called the "Son" of the Most High. The Lord God will give Him "the throne" of His Father "David"; He will "rule" over the house of Jacob "forever," and "there will be no end to His Kingdom . . ."* But the scandalous character of the Incarnation begins with this announcement: From now on, we find glory in humiliation, fullness in emptiness, riches in poverty, life in death. This is what St. Paul means when, speaking of the Incarnation, he says that the Word came in the flesh of sin, under the law, in the form of a slave, and under the power of death. His failure and His death agony begin already when He is received by Mary. At that moment, the descent and the kenosis truly begin for Him. The cross becomes His throne.

God wanted to put Himself in those things so that we might find Him in them. The desert wasteland of our human existence, our poverty and weakness, our sickness, our incarceration in darkness, our life on a dead-end street right in the midst of death —these things are now basically filled with the truth of His life, with His freedom that is true freedom, with the majesty of His power. We do not have to seek God any more in His unattainable otherness. He is right where we are. He is looking at us from every point of the compass. He is carrying our burden, has tasted the bitterness of our life, has travelled our streets, and meets us in the brothers and sisters of our own race. But that the saving victory of God's grace is concealed within our weakness so that it really confirms our distressing situation—we do not want to put up with that! Certainly, we would like to see the Incarnation of God, but in such a way that by means of it we can escape our ennui. However, it just so happens that Christian existence means being called to a life of scandal—the scandal of His coming in our flesh, and the paradox of achieving glory only through the kenosis of the cross.

From the moment of the Annunciation, Mary is intimately affected by this tension. Her fate is the same as that of her child! —not only in glory, but especially in labors, insults, and death. To be sure, the angel greets her as one perfectly graced, so that her heart is filled with the joy that she sings forth in her *Magnificat*. But at the same time, her great favor of grace has its bitterly serious side. Through this grace, she became the Mother of Sorrows. From the moment she utters her "Yes" to God's holy will, she becomes suspect, and, as it were, an outcast. And after she gave birth to her child, He Himself became a puzzle to her. She must even accept being abandoned by Him. But she accepted all of that when she answers the angel: *Behold, I am the handmaid of the Lord; let it be done to me according to your word.* (Lk. 1, 38)

KARL RAHNER [150]

173

April

St. Leo the Great
St. Justin Martyr
St. Mark
St. Catherine of Siena

APRIL 11
ST. LEO THE GREAT

On the death of Pope Sixtus III in 440, Leo, his archdeacon, was absent in Gaul on a diplomatic mission for the imperial government. Refusing to have anyone but him for their bishop, the Romans had him recalled by an official deputation and amidst general enthusiasm had him enthroned (440–461 A.D.).

The power of the Word.

Since in our Lord Jesus Christ, the true Son of God and man, we acknowledge a Divine nature from His Father, and a human substance from His Mother; although there is but one Person of God the Word and of the flesh, and both essences have acts in common, yet must we take notice of the character of the works themselves, and discern, by the gaze of a pure faith, to what heights the lowliness of infirmity is promoted, and to what depths the loftiness of power stoops down: what it is which the flesh does not without the Word, and what it is which the Word effects not without the flesh. For without the power of the Word, the Virgin would neither conceive nor bear; and without the reality of the flesh, the Infant would not lie wrapt in swathing bands. Without the power of the Word, the Magi would not adore a Child made known to them by a new star; and without the reality of the flesh, there would be no command to remove into Egypt the Child Whom Herod was desiring to kill. Without the power of the Word, the Father's voice sent forth from heaven would not say, *This is My beloved Son, in Whom I am well pleased* [Mt. 3, 17], and without the reality of the flesh, John would not bear witness, *Behold the Lamb of God, behold Him Who takes away the sins of the world.* [Jn. 1, 29] Without the power of the Word, there would not take place the recovery of the weakly and the revival of the dead; and without the reality of the flesh, He would not need food after fasting, nor sleep after weariness. Lastly, without the power of the Word, the Lord would not declare Himself equal to the Father; and without the reality of the flesh the Self-

same would not call the Father greater than Himself; while the
Catholic Faith accepts both statements and defends both, be-
lieving the one Son of God to be both Man and the Word, according to the distinctness of the Divine and human substance.
Much is there, dearly beloved, which we might take out of the
whole body of the Scriptures in order to expound this faith which
we preach: for nothing is oftener presented to us in the Divine
oracles, than the Son of God, as touching His Godhead, everlasting from the Father, and the Selfsame, as touching the flesh, born
in time from His Mother.

ST. LEO THE GREAT [151]

Doctor of the Church.

Through his eminent virtue, through his wisdom, through his
tireless zeal, he merited from the ancients the name of Leo the
Great. The superiority of his doctrine in illustrating the highest
mysteries of our Faith, in defending those mysteries against the
rise of errors and in formulating disciplinary and moral directives
(to say nothing of the singular majesty and richness of his
priestly eloquence), stands out to such a degree and is so distinguished (as is obvious from the praise of so many men and from
the enthusiastic exaltations of the councils, the Fathers and ecclesiastical writers), that a Pontiff of such great wisdom is absolutely not to be placed second in fame and esteem to any of the
holy Doctors who flourished in the Church.

BENEDICT XIV [152]

APRIL 14
ST. JUSTIN MARTYR

*Justin may be considered the first Christian philosopher and the
greatest of the early apologists. Born at Flavia Neapolis (Na-
blus) in Palestine around 100 A.D. of pagan parents, Justin became a Christian when he was 32 years old.*

"If these philosophers," I asked, "do not know the truth, what
teacher or method shall one follow?"

176

"A long time ago," he replied, "long before the time of those reputed philosophers, there lived blessed men who were just and loved by God, men who spoke through the inspiration of the Holy Spirit and predicted events that would take place in the future, which events are now taking place. We call these men the Prophets. They alone knew the truth and communicated it to men, whom they neither deferred to nor feared. With no desire for personal glory, they reiterated only what they heard and saw when inspired by the Holy Spirit. Their writings are still extant, and whoever reads them with the proper faith will profit greatly in his knowledge of the origin and end of things, and of any other matter that a philosopher should know. In their writings they gave no proof at that time of their statements, for, as reliable witnesses of the truth, they were beyond proof; but the happenings that have taken place and are now taking place force you to believe their words. They also are worthy of belief because of the miracles which they performed, for they exalted God, the Father and Creator of all things, and made known Christ, His Son, who was sent by Him. This the false prophets, who are filled with an erring and unclean spirit, have never done nor even do now, but they undertake to perform certain wonders to astound men and they glorify the demons and spirits of error. Above all, beseech God to open you the gates of light, for no one can perceive or understand these truths unless he has been enlightened by God and His Christ."

When he had said these and many other things which it is not now the fitting time to tell, he went his way, after admonishing me to meditate on what he had told me, and I never saw him again. But my spirit was immediately set on fire, and an affection for the prophets, and for those who are friends of Christ, took hold of me; while pondering on his words, I discovered that his was the only sure and useful philosophy.

ST. JUSTIN MARTYR [153]

The fruits of faith.

We who once reveled in impurities now cling to purity; we who devoted ourselves to the arts of magic now consecrate ourselves

177

to the good and unbegotten God; we who loved above all else the ways of acquiring riches and possessions now hand over to a community fund what we possess, and share it with every needy person; we who hated and killed one another and would not share our hearth with those of another tribe because of their different customs, now, after the coming of Christ, live together with them, and pray for our enemies, and try to convince those who hate us unjustly, so that they who live according to the good commands of Christ may have a firm hope of receiving the same reward as ourselves from God who governs all.

ST. JUSTIN MARTYR [154]

Martyrdom is the great proof of Christian faith.

No one can frighten or subdue us who believe in Jesus throughout the whole world. Although we are beheaded and crucified, and exposed to wild beasts and chains and flames, and every other means of torture, it is evident that we will not retract our profession of faith; the more we are persecuted, the more do others in ever-increasing numbers embrace the faith and become worshippers of God through the name of Jesus. Just as when one cuts off the fruit-bearing branches of the vine, it grows again and other blossoming and fruitful branches spring forth, so it is with us Christians. For the vine planted by God and Christ the Redeemer is His people.

ST. JUSTIN MARTYR [155]

There was no one who believed so much in Socrates as to die for his teaching, but not only philosophers and scholars believed in Christ, . . . but also workmen and men wholly uneducated, who all scorned glory, and fear, and death.

ST. JUSTIN MARTYR [156]

When he was an old man Justin and six fellow Christians were arrested (165 A.D.), *brought before Junius Rusticus, the prefect of the city, and ordered to sacrifice to the gods as a kind*

178

of loyalty oath. After bearing witness to his faith in the living God and in his son Jesus, Justin was questioned further.

Rusticus the prefect said, "Where do you assemble?" Justin said, "Where each one chooses and can; for do you fancy that we all meet in the very same place? Not so; because the God of the Christians is not circumscribed by place; but being invisible, fills heaven and earth, and everywhere is worshipped and glorified by the faithful." Rusticus the prefect said, "Tell me where you assemble, or into what place do you collect your followers?" Justin said, "I live above one Martinus, at the Timiotinian Bath; and during the whole time (and I am now living in Rome for the second time) I am unaware of any other meeting than his. And if any one wished to come to me, I communicated to him the doctrines of truth." Rusticus said, "Are you not, then, a Christian?" Justin said, "Yes, I am a Christian."

The prefect says to Justin, "Hearken, you who are called learned, and think that you know true doctrines; if you are scourged and beheaded, do you believe you will ascend into heaven?" Justin said, "I hope that, if I endure these things, I shall have His gifts. For I know that, to all who have thus lived, there abides the divine favour until the completion of the whole world." Rusticus the prefect said, "Do you suppose, then, that you will ascend into heaven to receive some recompense?" Justin said, "I do not suppose it, but I know and am fully persuaded of it." Rusticus the prefect said, "Let us, then, now come to the matter in hand, and which presses. Having come together, offer sacrifice with one accord to the gods." Justin said, "No right-thinking person falls away from piety to impiety." Rusticus the prefect said, "Unless you obey, you shall be mercilessly punished." Justin said, "Through prayer we can be saved on account of our Lord Jesus Christ, even when we have been punished, because this shall become to us salvation and confidence at the more fearful and universal judgment seat of our Lord and Saviour." Thus also said the other martyrs: "Do what you will, for we are Christians, and do not sacrifice to idols."

Rusticus the prefect pronounced sentence, saying, "Let those who have refused to sacrifice to the gods and to yield to the command of the emperor be scourged, and led away to suffer the

179

punishment of decapitation, according to the laws." The holy martyrs having glorified God, and having gone forth to the accustomed place, were beheaded, and perfected their testimony in the confession of the Saviour. And some of the faithful having secretly removed their bodies, laid them in a suitable place, the grace of our Lord Jesus Christ having wrought along with them, to whom be glory for ever and ever. Amen.

MARTYRDOM OF ST. JUSTIN [157]

APRIL 25
ST. MARK

You raised blessed Mark to the dignity of a preacher of the Good News. (Collect)

Under the reign of Claudius, by the benign and gracious providence of God, Peter, that powerful and great apostle, who by his courage took the lead of all the rest, was conducted to Rome. . . . He, like a noble commander of God, fortified with divine armour, bore the precious merchandise of the revealed light from the east to those in the west, announcing the light itself, and the salutary doctrine of the soul, the proclamation of the kingdom of God. . . .

So greatly did the splendour of piety enlighten the minds of Peter's hearers, that it was not sufficient to hear but once, nor to receive the unwritten doctrine of the gospel of God, but they persevered in every variety of entreaties, to solicit Mark as the companion of Peter, and whose Gospel we have, that he should leave them a monument of the doctrine thus orally communicated, in writing. Nor did they cease their solicitations until they had prevailed with the man, and thus become the means of that history which is called the Gospel according to Mark. They say also, that the apostle [Peter], having ascertained what was done by the revelation of the Spirit, was delighted with the zealous ardour expressed by these men, and that the history obtained his authority for the purpose of being read in the churches.

EUSEBIUS [158]

180

To preach again the unknown God we must use the same means as those who preached Him for the first time. And their weapons were these:

Prayer.

Mortification.

Work.

Thirst for souls.

Joy and optimism of the sons of God.

Union with the head, Peter, Rome.

J. URTEAGA [159]

According to our Lord's announcements before the event, Christianity was to prevail and to become a great empire, and to fill the earth; but it was to accomplish this destiny, not as other victorious powers had done, and as the Jews expected, by force of arms or by other means of this world, but by the novel expedient of sanctity and suffering. If some aspiring party of this day, the great Orleans family, or a branch of the Hohenzollern, wishing to found a kingdom, were to profess, as their only weapon, the practice of virtue, they would not startle us more than it startled a Jew eighteen hundred years ago, to be told that his glorious Messiah was not to fight, like Joshua or David, but simply to preach. It is indeed a thought so strange, both in its prediction and in its fulfilment, as urgently to suggest to us that some Divine Power went with him who conceived and proclaimed it.

JOHN HENRY NEWMAN [160]

APRIL 30

ST. CATHERINE OF SIENA

Catherine Benincasa (1347–1380) was the twenty-fourth child of a garrulous family of cloth-dyers. Catherine the mystic and intimate friend of God never learned to read and write, but she came to exercise an enormous influence in the life of the fourteenth-century Church. It was she who persuaded Pope Gregory XI to return to Rome from his Avignon exile. She it was who worked desperately during the last year of her life to heal the papal

181

schism which was to do such damage to the late medieval Church.

As the "mother" of a spiritual family of men and women, clerics and lay people, she was moved to leave behind her an incomparable spiritual treasury of letters of spiritual direction and exhortation. Only The Dialogue, *a series of colloquies between God the Father and Catherine, surpasses the quality of her letters.*

Catherine writes to Brother Raymond of Capua, O.P., her confessor, of how she rescued a young Sienese nobleman, condemned to death for criticizing the government of the Republic, from the unbelief and black despair which was destroying him.

I have just received a head in my hands, which was to me of such sweetness as heart cannot think, nor tongue say, nor eye see, nor the ears hear. . . . I went to visit him whom you know: whence he received such comfort and consolation that he confessed, and prepared himself very well. And he made me promise by the love of God that when the time of the sentence should come, I would be with him. So I promised, and did. Then in the morning, before the bell rang, I went to him: and he received great consolation. I led him to hear Mass, and he received the Holy Communion, which he had never before received. His will was accorded and submitted to the will of God; and only one fear was left, that of not being strong at the moment [of death]. But the measureless and glowing goodness of God deceived him, creating in him such affection and love in the desire of God that he did not know how to abide without Him, and said: "Stay with me, and do not abandon me. So it shall not be otherwise than well with me. And I die content." And he held his head upon my breast. I heard then the rejoicing, and breathed the fragrance of his blood; and it was not without the fragrance of mine, which I desire to shed for the sweet Bridegroom Jesus. And, desire waxing in my soul, feeling his fear, I said: "Comfort thee, sweet my brother; since we shall soon arrive at the Wedding Feast. Thou shalt go there bathed in the sweet Blood of the Son of God, with the sweet Name of Jesus, which I will never to leave thy memory. And I await thee at the place of justice." Now think, father and son, his heart then lost all fear, and his face changed from sorrow to gladness; and he rejoiced, he exulted, and said: "Whence comes such grace to me, that the sweetness of my soul will await me at the holy place of justice?" See, that he had come to so much light that he called the place of justice holy! And he said: "I shall go wholly joyous, and strong, and it will seem to me a thousand years before I arrive, thinking that you are awaiting me there." And he said words so sweet as to break one's heart, of the goodness of God.

I waited for him then at the place of justice; and waited there with constant prayer, in the presence of Mary and of Catherine, Virgin and martyr. But before I attained, I prostrated me and stretched my neck upon the block; but my desire did not come there, for I had too full consciousness of myself. Then up! I prayed, I constrained her, I cried "Mary!" for I wished this grace, that at the moment of death she should give him a light and a peace in his heart, and then I should see him reach his goal. Then my soul became so full that although a multitude of people were there, I could see no human creature, for the sweet promise made to me.

Then he came, like a gentle lamb; and seeing me, he began to smile, and wanted me to make the sign of the Cross. When he had received the sign, I said: "Down! To the Bridal, sweetest my brother! For soon shalt thou be in the enduring life." He prostrated him with great gentleness, and I stretched out his neck; and bowed me down, and recalled to him the Blood of the Lamb. His lips said naught save Jesus! and, Catherine! And so saying, I received his head in my hands, closing my eyes in the Divine Goodness, and saying, "I will!"

ST. CATHERINE OF SIENA [161]

Catherine rebukes and exhorts the dilatory Gregory XI in a brief and powerful summary of her oft-reiterated pleas. "It is surely one of the most surprising letters ever written by a devout and wholly faithful subject to her acknowledged head."

Most holy and sweet father, your poor unworthy daughter Catherine in Christ sweet Jesus, commends herself to you in His precious Blood: with desire to see you a manly man, free from

183

any fear of fleshly love toward yourself, or toward any creature related to you in the flesh; since I perceive in the sweet Presence of God that nothing so hinders your holy, good desire and so serves to hinder the honour of God and the exaltation and reform of Holy Church, as this. Therefore, my soul desires with immeasurable love that God by His infinite mercy may take from you all passion and lukewarmness of heart, and re-form you another man, by forming in you anew a burning and ardent desire; for in no other way could you fulfil the will of God and the desire of His servants. Alas, alas, sweetest "Babbo" mine, pardon my presumption in what I have said to you and am saying; I am constrained by the Sweet Primal Truth to say it. His will, father, is this, and thus demands of you. It demands that you execute justice on the abundance of many iniquities committed by those who are fed and pastured in the garden of Holy Church; declaring that brutes should not be fed with the food of men. Since He has given you authority and you have assured it, you should use your virtue and power: and if you are not willing to use it, it would be better for you to resign what you have assumed; more honour to God and health to your soul would it be. . . .

Beware, as you hold your life dear, that you commit no negligence in this, nor treat as jests the works of the Holy Spirit, which are demanded from you because you can do them. If you want justice, you can execute it. You can have peace, withdrawing from the perverse pomps and delights of the world, preserving only the honour of God and the due of Holy Church. Authority also you have to give peace to those who ask you for it. Then, since you are not poor but rich—you who bear in your hand the keys of Heaven, to whom you open it is open, and to whom you shut it is shut—if you do not do this, you would be rebuked by God. I, if I were in your place, should fear lest divine judgment come upon me. Therefore I beg you most gently on behalf of Christ crucified to be obedient to the will of God, for I know that you want and desire no other thing than to do His will, that this sharp rebuke fall not upon you: "Cursed be thou, for the time and the strength entrusted to thee thou hast not used." I believe, father, by the goodness of God, and also taking hope from your holiness, that you will so act that this will not fall upon you.

I say no more. Pardon me, pardon me; for the great love which I bear to your salvation, and my great grief when I see the contrary, makes me speak so. Willingly would I have said it to your own person, fully to unburden my conscience. When it shall please your Holiness that I come to you, I will come willingly. So do that I may not appeal to Christ crucified from you; for to no other can I appeal, for there is no greater on earth. Remain in the holy and sweet grace of God. I ask you humbly for your benediction. Sweet Jesus, Jesus Love.

ST. CATHERINE OF SIENA [162]

May

St. Joseph
St. Athanasius
St. Monica
Sts. Philip and James
St. Philip Neri
St. Augustine of Canterbury

ST. JOSEPH

He is the man on the outskirts, standing in the shadows, silently waiting, there when wanted and always ready to help. He is the man in whose life God is constantly intervening with warnings and visions. Without complaint he allows his own plans to be set aside. His life is a succession of prophecies and dream-messages, of packing up and moving on. He is the man who dreams of setting up a quiet household, simply leading a decent home life and going about his everyday affairs, attending to his business and worshiping God and who, instead, is condemned to a life of wondering. Beset with doubts, heavy-hearted and uneasy in his mind, his whole life disrupted, he has to take to the open road, to make his way through an unfriendly country finding no shelter but a miserable stable for those he holds most dear. He is the man who sets aside all thought of self and shoulders his responsibilities bravely—and obeys.

His message is willing obedience. He is the man who serves. It never enters his head to question God's commands; he makes all the necessary preparations and is ready when God's call comes. Willing, unquestioning service is the secret of his life. It is his message for us and his judgment of us. How proud and presumptuous and self-sufficient we are. We have crabbed and confined God within the pitiable limits of our obstinacy, our complacency, our opportunism, our mania for "self-expression." We have given God—and with him everything that is noble and spiritual and holy—only the minimum of recognition, only as much as would serve to flatter our self-esteem and further self-will. Just how wrong this is life itself has shown us since in consequence of our attitude we have come to abject bondage dominated by ruthless states which force the individual to sink his identity in the common mass and give his service whether he wishes or not. The prayer of St. Paul—*do with me what thou wilt*—the quiet and willing readiness to serve of the man Joseph, could lead us to a truer and more genuine freedom.

ALFRED DELP [163]

O St. Joseph, guardian of Jesus, chaste spouse of Mary, you who spent your life in the perfect accomplishment of duty, maintaining with the work of your hands the Holy Family of Nazareth, grant your kind protection to those who, full of trust, turn to you now! You know their desires, their difficulties, their hopes; they pray to you because they know that in you they find one who understands and protects them. You also have known trials, toil, and fatigue; yet, in the midst of the material cares of life, your soul, full of the most profound peace, rejoiced with indescribable happiness in the close companionship of the Son of God who was entrusted to your care, and of Mary, his sweet Mother. May those whom you protect understand that they are not alone in their toil: may they perceive Jesus by their side, receive him with grace and guard him faithfully, as you did. And with your prayers obtain that in every family, in every factory or work room, and wherever a Christian works, everything may be sanctified in charity, patience, and justice, and in the search for righteousness, so that the gifts of heavenly love may be showered upon them.

JOHN XXIII [164]

Jesus sanctified labor, not by endowing it with technical perfection, but by performing it out of love, just as He did not bring us science, art, philosophy, or even principally an ethic, but the love that should lie at the source and foundation of all these things.

The fact that Jesus performed such a primitive kind of work in such lowly conditions certainly does not give us motives for devoutly opposing technology or refusing to fight for the just rights of the worker. Our Lord's life in Nazareth teaches us that all those things, inventions, plannings, the betterment of social conditions, are valuable only if they are animated by the love He teaches and communicates to us. Christ's love does not merely inspire our labor, making us willing to suffer poverty and contempt—although this lesson is also contained in it—but it also

teaches earnest and faithful professional service of our fellow-
man.

PETER SCHOONENBERG [165]

MAY 2
ST. ATHANASIUS

*Born around 296, and as a young man a deacon of the Patriarch
Alexander of Alexandria, Athanasius soon became embroiled in
the great theological dispute of the fourth century. A leader
in the first Ecumenical Council of Nicea in 325, he participated in
the condemnation of Arius, who was attempting to rob Christ of
his divinity, and later as Patriarch of Alexandria (328–373), he
spent a lifetime combatting this persistent heresy.*

*"Perfect God and perfect man"—God and man in the full
sense of these terms. Because Athanasius knew that man's salvation depended on the truth of these assertions, he passed almost
his whole career fighting for orthodoxy.*

Of old time He [the Word] was wont to come to the Saints individually, and to hallow those who truly received Him; but
neither, on their birth, was it said that He had become man, nor,
when they suffered, was it said that He himself suffered. But when
He came among us from Mary, once for all in fulness of the ages,
for the abolition of sin (for so it was pleasing to the Father to
send His own Son, *made of a woman, made under the Law*
[Gal. 4, 4]), then it is said, that He took flesh and became man,
and in that flesh He suffered for us (as Peter says, *Christ therefore having suffered for us in the flesh* [1 Pet. 4, 1]), that it
might be shown, and that we all might believe, that, whereas
He was ever God, and hallowed those to whom He came, and
ordered all things according to the Father's will, afterwards
for our sakes He became man, and *bodily,* as the Apostle says,
the Godhead dwelt in the flesh; as much as to say, "Being God,
He had His own body, and using this as an instrument, He became man for our sakes."

And on account of this, the properties of the flesh are said to be His, since He was in it, such as to hunger, to thirst, to suffer, to weary, and the like, of which the flesh is capable; while on the other hand the works proper to the Word Himself, such as to raise the dead, to restore sight to the blind, and to cure the woman with an issue of blood, He did through His own body, and the Word bore the infirmities of the flesh, as His own, for His was the flesh; and the flesh ministered to the works of the Godhead, because the Godhead was in it, for the body was God's. And well has the Prophet said *carried;* and has not said, "He tended our infirmities," lest, as being external to the body, and only healing it, as He has always done, He should leave men subject still to death; but He *carries* our infirmities, and He himself bears our sins, that it might be shown that He became man for us, and that the body which in Him bore them was His proper body; and, while He received no hurt Himself by *bearing our sins in His body on the tree,* as Peter speaks [1 Pet. 2, 24], we men were redeemed from our own affections, and were filled with the righteousness of the Word. Whence it was that, when the flesh suffered, the Word was not external to it; and therefore is the passion said to be His; and when He did divinely His Father's works, the flesh was not external to Him, but in the body itself did the Lord do them. Hence, when made man, He said, *If I do not the works of the Father, believe Me not; but if I do, though you believe not Me, believe the works, that you may know that the Father is in Me, and I in Him.* [Jn. 10, 37–38]

And thus when there was need to raise Peter's wife's mother who was sick of a fever, He stretched forth His hand humanly, but He stopped the illness divinely. And in the case of the man blind from the birth, human was the spittle which He gave forth from the flesh, but divinely did He open the eyes through the clay. And in the case of Lazarus, He gave forth a human voice, as man; but divinely, as God, did He raise Lazarus from the dead. These things were so done, were so manifested, because He had a body, not in appearance, but in truth; and it beseemed that the Lord, in putting on human flesh, should put it on whole with the affections proper to it; that, as we say that the body was proper to Him so also we may say that the affections of the body were absolutely proper to Him, though they did not touch Him accord-

190

ing to His Godhead. If then the body had been another's, to that other too had been the affections attributed; but if the flesh is the Word's (for *the Word became flesh* [Jn. 1, 14]), of necessity then the affections also of the flesh are ascribed to Him, whose the flesh is. And to whom the bodily affections are ascribed, such namely as to be condemned, to be scourged, to thirst, and the cross, and death, and the other infirmities of the body, of Him too is the triumph and the grace. For this cause then, consistently and fittingly such affections are ascribed not to another, but to the Lord; that the grace also may be from Him, and that we may become, not worshippers of any other, but truly devout towards God, because we invoke no creature, no ordinary man, but the natural and true Son from God, who has become man, yet is not the less Lord and God and Saviour.

ST. ATHANASIUS [166]

The Word took flesh to insure man's redemption and deification.

For therefore did He assume the body created and human, that having renewed it as its Framer, He might deify it in Himself, and thus might introduce us all into the kingdom of heaven after His likeness. For man had not been made god anew if joined to a creature, nor unless the Son were very God; nor had man stood in the Father's presence unless it had been His natural and true Word who stood clad in that body which belonged to man. And, as we had not been freed from sin and the curse, had it not been human flesh in its nature which the Word put on, (for we should have had nothing common with what was foreign), so also man had not been made god, unless the Word who became man had in His nature been from the Father and true and proper to Him. For therefore was the union such, in order that He might unite what is man by nature to Him who is in the nature of the Godhead, and man's salvation and deification might be sure.

ST. ATHANASIUS [167]

MAY 4
ST. MONICA

Monica's only life is to be found in the Confessions *of her son Augustine. There she is with her defects as well as her qualities, no plaster saint but a real person.*

Monica was a Christian wife and mother married to a pagan husband of sometimes savage temper and with a son of great promise turned sensualist and the devotee of heresy. A woman very much of her own time and place, trying hard to live her faith in the eyes of all, she succeeded in her apostolate of kindness and prayer in winning over both her husband and her son.

She was brought up in a modest, sober way. It was you who made her obedient to her parents rather than her parents who made her obedient to you. And when she reached marriageable age she was given to a husband whom she served as her master. She tried to win him to you, preaching you to him by the beauty of the character which you had given her and by which you made her able to provoke love and respect and the admiration of her husband. So she endured his infidelities and never had a single quarrel with him on this subject. She was waiting for your mercy to be shown upon him so that he might believe in you and be made chaste. He, in fact, though an extremely kind man by nature, was also very hot-tempered. But my mother knew that an angry husband must not be contradicted, not in deed nor even in word. Only when he had calmed down and become quiet would she, when she saw her opportunity, explain to him the reasons for what she had done, if he had happened to fly into a rage for no good reason. Indeed there were many wives with husbands much milder than hers who went about with their faces disfigured by the marks of blows, and when they got together to talk they would often complain of the way their husbands behaved. But my mother, speaking lightly but giving serious advice, used to say that the fault was in their tongues. They had all heard, she said, the marriage contract read out to them and from that day they ought to regard it as a legal instrument by which they were made servants; so they should remember their station and not set themselves up against their masters. And they, knowing what a violent husband she had to put up with, were amazed that it had never been heard of nor had there been any evidence to show that Patricius had ever beaten his wife or that there had been a family quarrel that had lasted as much as a single day. They asked her in confidence how she managed it, and she told them her rule, which was as I have described. Those who followed it found that they had every reason to thank her for it; those who did not were still bullied and kept under.

There was a time when her mother-in-law had been angry with her. This had all started because of the whispering of malicious servants. But my mother showed such a respectful attitude to her and so won her over by her constant patience and forbearance that she went herself to her son, told him the names of those whose interfering tongues were disturbing the domestic peace between her and her daughter-in-law and demanded that those concerned should be punished. Then out of deference to his mother, care for good order in the household, and consideration for peace in his own family he had the servants whose names had been given to him beaten, as his mother had asked, and she told them that this was the reward that any of them else might expect from her if they tried to please her by speaking ill of her daughter-in-law. None of them ventured to do so after that, and they lived together in future on the most remarkably happy and kind terms. . . .

Finally, toward the very end of his earthly life, she won her husband over to you, and now that he was a believer she no longer lamented in him the things which she had put up with in him before he was converted. She was also the servant of your servants. All of them who knew her found in her good reason to praise and honor and love you, because on the evidence of the fruit of her holy conversation they could feel your presence in her heart. For she had been the wife of one man, had requited her parents, had governed her house piously, was well reported of for good works, had brought up children, as often travailing in birth of them as she saw them straying away from you. Finally, Lord—since it is by your gift that we are allowed to speak—with

193

regard to all of us your servants who, before she went to sleep in you, were living together after receiving the grace of baptism, she gave to each one of us the care that a mother gives to her son and to each one of us the service which a daughter gives to her father. . . .

One day while she was ill she had a fainting fit and temporarily lost consciousness of her surroundings. We hurried to her side, but she soon regained consciousness, and, seeing my brother and me standing by her, she said to us, as though she were trying to find the answer to some question, "Where am I?" Then, as we stood dumb with grief, she looked in our faces and said: "Here you will bury your mother." I remained quiet and kept back my tears; but my brother said something to her to the effect that he hoped that she would have the good fortune to die in her own country and not abroad. On hearing this an anxious expression came over her face, and she gave him a reproachful look for still savoring of such earthly things. Then she looked into my face and said: "See what he is saying!" Soon afterward she said to both of us, "You may lay this body of mine anywhere. Do not worry at all about that. All I ask you is this, that wherever you may be you will remember me at the altar of the Lord." . . .

And so on the ninth day of her illness, in the fifty-sixth year of her age and the thirty-third of mine, that devout and holy soul was freed from the body. I closed her eyes, and a great flood of sorrow swept into my heart and would have overflowed in tears. But my eyes obeyed the forcible dictate of my mind and seemed to drink that fountain dry. Terrible indeed was my state as I struggled so. . . .

And then little by little my former thoughts of your handmaid returned. I remembered how devoutly and with what holiness she conducted herself in your sight, how kind and considerate she was to us. And now suddenly I had lost all this. With you seeing me I found solace in weeping for her and for myself, on her behalf and on my own. So I allowed the tears which I had been holding back to fall, and I let them flow as they would, making them a pillow for my heart, and my heart rested on them, for only your ears could hear my lament and not the ears of some man who might have given a wrong or contemptuous in-

194

terpretation of it. And now, Lord, I am confessing this to you in writing and anyone who cares can read what I have written and interpret it as he likes, and if he finds that I did wrong in weeping during this small portion of an hour for my mother—a mother who for the time was dead to my eyes and who for so many years had wept for me, that I might live in your eyes—let him not despise me; let him rather, if he is a man of great charity, himself weep for my sins to you, the Father of all the brethren of your Christ. . . .

So let her rest in peace with her husband, than whom she had no other husband either before or after; whom she obeyed, with patience bringing forth fruit for you, so that she might win him for you also. And inspire, my Lord and my God, inspire your servants my brethren, your sons my masters, whom I serve with heart and voice and pen, that as many as shall read this may remember at your altar Monica, your servant, with Patricius, her husband, through whose flesh you brought me into this life, though how I do not know. May they with holy affection remember those two who were my parents in this transitory light, who are my brethren under you, Our Father, in our Catholic mother, and my fellow citizens in the eternal Jerusalem for which your people in their pilgrimage sigh from the beginning of their journey until their return home. And so by means of these Confessions of mine I pray that my mother may have her last request of me still more richly answered in the prayers of many others besides myself.

ST. AUGUSTINE [168]

MAY 11
STS. PHILIP AND JAMES

Under a celestial influence and co-operation, the doctrine of the Saviour, like the rays of the sun, quickly irradiated the whole world. Presently, in accordance with divine prophecy, the sound of his inspired evangelists and apostles had gone throughout all the earth, and their words to the ends of the world. Throughout every city and village, like a replenished barn-floor, churches were rapidly found abounding, and filled with members from every people. Those who, in consequence of the delusions that had descended to them from their ancestors, had been fettered by the ancient disease of idolatrous superstition, were now liberated, by the power of Christ, through the teachings and miracles of his messengers. And, as if delivered from dreadful masters, and emancipated from the most cruel bondage, they on the one hand renounced the whole multitude of gods and demons, and on the other, confessed that there was only one true God, the Creator of all things. This same God they now also honoured with the rites of a true piety, under the influence of that inspired and reasonable worship which had been planted among men by our Saviour.

EUSEBIUS [169]

I am the way, the truth, and the life. (Gospel)

Every one who learns any craft watches his master and sees how by his skill and his knowledge he executes the work of his craft; and he himself copies him and executes the work which he has set him, that he may not be ill spoken of by him. But if he abate anything of the (tasks) set him, he is not perfect. We, then, who have our Lord for master and teacher, why do not we imitate His teaching and His conversation? For He left riches and favour, and power and glory, and came thus in poverty; and moreover He parted with Mary His blessed mother, and with His brethren, and with His life itself, and endured persecution even unto the cross. And these things He endured for our sake, that He might redeem you also, who are of the People, from the bonds of the Second Legislation [the Old Law], of which we have already spoken, and might redeem you also, who are of the Gentiles, from the worship of idols and from all ungodliness, and get you for an inheritance. If then He suffered thus for our sake, to redeem us who believe in Him, and was not ashamed, why do not we also imitate His sufferings, while He gives us endurance?—and this for our own sake, that we may be delivered from the death of fire. For He endured for our sake, but we for our own sake. Or has our Lord any need that we should suffer for Him? Rather it is this alone that He desires, to make proof of

196

the love of our faith, and of our free will. Let us then part with our parents and our kinsfolk, and with all that is in this world, and even with our life.

We must indeed pray that we come not into temptation; yet if we be called to martyrdom, let us confess when we are interrogated, and when we suffer let us endure, and when we are afflicted let us rejoice, and when we are persecuted let us not grieve; for so doing, not only shall we deliver ourselves from hell, but we shall also teach those who are young in the faith, and the hearers, to do the like: and they shall live before God. But if we fail in faith towards the Lord, and deny through the infirmity of the body—as our Lord said: *The spirit is willing and ready, but the body is weak* [Mt. 26, 41] —we shall not only destroy ourselves, but shall kill also our brethren with us. For when they see our denial, they will think that they have been made disciples of an erring doctrine; and when they stumble, we shall render an account for them as well as for ourselves, every one of us, to the Lord in the day of Judgment.

But if thou be taken and brought before the authority, and deny the hope that thou hast towards the Lord by thy holy faith, and thou be set at large to-day, but to-morrow fall sick of a fever and take to thy bed; or if thy stomach ail thee and retain no food, but vomit it out with grievous pains; or thou be afflicted with a disease of the belly, or with a disease in one of thy members; or thou bring up blood and bile from within thee by reason of dire disorders; or thou have an ulcer in one of thy members and be cut by the hands of physicians, and die in manifold afflictions and torments: what then will thy denial have availed thee which thou hast denied, O man? For behold, thy soul has inherited pains and afflictions, and thou hast destroyed thy life for ever before God; and thou shalt burn and be tormented without respite everlastingly: even as the Lord has said: *Every one that loves his life, shall lose it; and everyone that shall lose his life for my sake, shall find it.* [Jn. 12, 25]

DIDASCALIA APOSTOLORUM [170]

197

ST. PHILIP NERI

By his quiet but radiant joy, his simplicity and persistent zeal, and his skill in spiritual direction, Philip Neri (1515–1595) became the Apostle of Rome and the founder of the Roman Oratory.

It is not surprising that, with this tenderness, with this prudence, and with the zeal and charity to which both were subordinate, his influence increased year by year, till he gained a place in the heart of the Roman population, which he has never lost. There are those whose greatest works are their earliest; there are others, who, at first scarcely distinguishable from a whole class who look the same, distance them in the long run, and do more and more wonderful works the longer they live. Philip was thirty-five before he was ordained; forty, before he began his exercises in his room; fifty, before he had a church; sixty before he formed his disciples into a congregation; near seventy, before he put himself at the head of it. As the Blessed Virgin's name has by a majestic growth expanded and extended itself through the Church, *taking root in an honourable people, and resting in the Holy City* [Ecclus. 24, 13], so the influence of Philip was, at the end of many years, paramount in that place which he had so long dwelt in as an obscure, disregarded stranger. Sharp eyes and holy sympathies indeed had detected "Philip Neri, as a saint living in caves," when he was a youth; but it required half a century to develop this truth to the intelligence of the multitude of men. At length there was no possibility of mistaking it. Visitors to Rome discerned the presence of one who was greater than Pope and Cardinals, holy, venerable and vigilant as the rulers of the Church then were. "Among all the wonderful things which I saw in Rome," says one of them, writing when Philip was turned fifty, "I took the chief pleasure in beholding the multitude of devout and spiritual persons who frequented the Oratory. Amid the monuments of antiquity, the superb palaces and courts of so many illustrious lords, it appeared to me that the glory of this exemplar shone forth with surpassing light." "I go," says another visitor, ten years later, "to the Oratory, where they deliver every day most beautiful discourses on the gospel, or on the virtues and vices, or ecclesiastical history, or the lives of the saints. Persons of distinction go to hear them, bishops, prelates, and the like. They who deliver them are in holy orders, and of most exemplary life. Their superior is a certain Reverend Father Philip, an old man of sixty, who, they say, is an oracle, not only in Rome, but in the far-off parts of Italy, and of France and Spain so that many come to him for counsel; indeed he is another Thomas à Kempis, or Tauler."

But it required to live in Rome to understand what his influence really was. Nothing was too high for him, nothing too low. He taught poor begging women to use mental prayer; he took out boys to play; he protected orphans; he acted as novice-master to the children of St. Dominic. He was the teacher and director of artisans, mechanics, cashiers in banks, merchants, workers in gold, artists, men of science. He was consulted by monks, canons, lawyers, physicians, courtiers; ladies of the highest rank, convicts going to execution, engaged in their turn his solicitude and prayers. Cardinals hung about his room, and Popes asked for his miraculous aid in disease, and his ministrations in death. It was his mission to save men, not from, but in, the world. To break the haughtiness of rank, and the fastidiousness of fashion, he gave his penitents public mortifications; to draw the young from the theatres, he opened his Oratory of Sacred Music; to rescue the careless from the Carnival and its excesses, he set out in pilgrimage to the Seven Basilicas. For those who loved reading, he substituted, for the works of chivalry or the hurtful novels of the day, the true romance and the celestial poetry of the Lives of the Saints. He set one of his disciples to write history against the heretics of that age; another to treat of the Notes of the Church; a third, to undertake the Martyrs and Christian Antiquities; —for, while in the discourses and devotions of the Oratory, he prescribed the simplicity of the primitive monks, he wished his children, individually and in private, to cultivate all their gifts to the full. He, however, was, after all and in all, their true model,—the humble priest, shrinking from every kind of dignity, or post, or office, and living the greater part of day and night in prayer, in his room or upon the housetop.

JOHN HENRY NEWMAN [171]

MAY 28

ST. AUGUSTINE OF CANTERBURY

Once partly Christian in Roman times the province of Britain suffered terrible physical and spiritual damage at the hands of Anglo-Saxon invaders during the fifth century. One of the missionary projects of Pope Gregory the Great was the sending of a band of Benedictine monks under the leadership of Prior Augustine to the southeastern Saxon kingdom of Kent in 596.

The papal mission to England.

Reassured by the encouragement of the blessed father Gregory, Augustine and his fellow-servants of Christ resumed their work in the word of God and arrived in Britain [A.D. 597]. The King of Kent at this time was the powerful King Ethelbert, whose domains extended northwards to the river Humber, which forms the boundary between the north and south Angles. To the east of Kent lies the large island of Thanet, . . . It was here that God's servant Augustine landed with companions, who are said to have been forty in number. At the direction of blessed Pope Gregory, they had brought interpreters from among the Franks, and they sent these to Ethelbert, saying that they came from Rome bearing very glad news, which infallibly assured all who would receive it of eternal joy in heaven, and an everlasting kingdom with the living and true God. On receiving this message, the king ordered them to remain in the island where they had landed, and gave directions that they were to be provided with all necessaries until he should decide what action to take. For he had already heard of the Christian religion, having a Christian wife of the Frankish royal house named Bertha, whom he had received from her parents on condition that she should have freedom to hold and practice her faith unhindered with Bishop Liudhard whom they had sent as her chaplain.

After some days, the king came to the island, and sitting down in the open air, summoned Augustine and his companions to an audience. But he took precautions that they should not approach him in a house, for he held an ancient superstition that if they were practisers of magical arts, they might have opportunity to deceive and master him. But the monks were endowed with power from God, not from the Devil, and approached the king carrying a silver cross as their standard, and the likeness of our Lord and Saviour painted on a board. First of all they offered prayer to God, singing a litany for the eternal salvation both of themselves and of those for whose sake they had come. And when, at the king's command, Augustine had sat down and preached the word of life to the king and his court, the king said: "Your words and promises are fair indeed, but they are new and strange to us, and I cannot accept them and abandon the age-old beliefs of the whole English nation. But since you have travelled far, and I can see that you are sincere in your desire to instruct us in what you believe to be true and excellent, we will not harm you. We will receive you hospitably, and take care to supply you with all that you need; nor will we forbid you to preach and win any people you can to your religion." The king then granted them a dwelling in the city of Canterbury, which was the chief city of all his realm, and in accordance with his promise, he allowed them provisions and did not withdraw their freedom to preach. Tradition says that as they approached the city, bearing the holy cross and the likeness of our great King and Lord Jesus Christ as was their custom, they sang in unison this litany: "We pray Thee, O Lord, in all Thy mercy, that Thy wrath and anger may be turned away from this city and from Thy holy house, for we are sinners. Alleluia."

As soon as they had occupied the house given to them they began to emulate the life of the apostles and the primitive Church. They were constantly at prayer; they fasted and kept vigils; they preached the word of life to whomsoever they could. They regarded worldly things as of little importance, and accepted only necessary food from those they taught. They practised what they preached, and were willing to endure any hardship, and even to die for the Faith which they proclaimed. A number of heathen, admiring the simplicity of their holy lives and the comfort of their heavenly message, believed and were baptized. On the east side of the city stood an old church, built in honour of Saint Martin during the Roman occupation of Britain, where the Christian queen went to pray. Here they first assembled to sing the psalms, to pray, to say Mass, to preach, and to baptize, until the king's own conversion to the Faith enabled them to preach openly, and to build and restore churches everywhere.

At length the king and others, edified by the pure lives of these holy men and their gracious promises, the truth of which they confirmed by many miracles, believed and were baptized. Thenceforward great numbers gathered each day to hear the word of God, forsaking their heathen rites, and entering the unity of Christ's holy Church as believers. While the king was pleased at their faith and conversion, he would not compel anyone to accept Christianity, for he had learned from his instructors and guides to salvation that the service of Christ must be accepted freely and not under compulsion; nevertheless, he showed greater favour to believers, because they were fellow-citizens of the kingdom of heaven. And it was not long before he granted his teachers a property of their own in his capital of Canterbury, and gave them possessions of various kinds to supply their wants.

ST. BEDE [172]

The Apostle to the English.

Gregory to Eulogius, bishop of Alexandria. . . . Since your good deeds bear fruit in which you rejoice as well as others, I am making you a return for benefits received by sending news of the same kind. And this is that whilst the people of the English, placed in a corner of the world, still remained without faith, worshipping stocks and stones, I resolved, aided in this by your prayers, that I ought with God's assistance to send to this people a monk [Augustine] from my monastery to preach. He, by licence given from me, was made bishop by the bishops of the Germanies and with their encouragement was brought on his way to the people aforesaid in the ends of the world; and already letters have reached us telling of his safety and of his work, that both he and they who were sent with him are radiant with such great miracles amongst this people, that they seem to reproduce the powers of the apostles in the signs that they display. Indeed, on the solemn feast of the Lord's Nativity now past, more than ten thousand Angles, according to our information, were baptized by the same our brother and fellow-bishop. I have told you this that you may know not only what you do among the people of Alexandria by speaking, but also what you accomplish in the ends of the world by prayer. For your prayers are in that place where you are not, whilst your holy deeds are exhibited in that place where you are.

ST. GREGORY THE GREAT [173]

June

St. Boniface

ST. BONIFACE

St. Boniface (680–754), an Englishman who later became the "Apostle of Germany," was the first missionary able to lay the foundations of a settled ecclesiastical organization for Germany. After the death of Charles Martel, Boniface was authorized by Pope Gregory III to carry through a reform of the whole Frankish Church, a task which he accomplished in a series of councils. In 747 he became Archbishop of Mainz, but resigned in a few years to return to Frisia, the scene of his first labors, where he met with martyrdom. His devotion to the papacy, coupled with the success of his work, greatly assisted the spread of papal influence.

Boniface describes to Bishop Daniel of Winchester the obstacles to his reform of the Frankish Church and the conversion of the heathen. (742–746)

To Bishop Daniel, beloved in the Lord, Boniface, a servant of the servants of God, affectionate greetings in Christ.

It is the usual custom for men who are in trouble and anxiety to seek the consolation and advice of those on whose wisdom and affection they can rely. And so it is with me. Relying on your friendship and your experience, I come to lay before you all my difficulties and vexations of mind and beg you to support me with your comfort and advice. To quote the Apostle, *all is conflict without and anxiety within;* but in my case there are also conflicts within and anxiety without. This is caused in particular by false priests and hypocrites who set God at defiance, thereby rushing to their own damnation and leading the faithful astray by their scandals and errors. They say, in the words of the prophet, *Peace, peace, but there is no peace.* They strive to sow cockle among the wheat, to choke with weeds or pervert into a poisonous weed the Word of God, which we received from the Catholic and Apostolic Church and which, to the best of our ability, we endeavour to disseminate. But what we plant they make no attempt to water in order that it may grow; in order, rather, that it may wither away they use every effort to root it out by proposing to the faithful new sects and new falsehoods. . . .

In our visits to the Frankish court to obtain assistance and protection, it is not possible, as required by canon law, wholly to avoid the company of such men. We are careful, however, not to communicate with them in the sacred body and blood of the Lord during the celebration of Mass. We also avoid taking their advice or asking their consent, for to such men, mixing with heathens and the common people, our toils and struggles are quite incomprehensible. When a priest, a deacon, a cleric or a monk, or any of the faithful, leaves the bosom of the Church, then he joins the heathens in abusing the members of the Church, and this raises terrible obstacles to the spread of the Gospel. . . .

As regards my contacts with the priests already mentioned, I am anxious to have and to follow your considered advice. Without the patronage of the Frankish prince I can neither govern the faithful of the Church nor protect the priests, clerics, monks and nuns of God, nor can I forbid the practice of heathen rites and the worship of idols in Germany without his orders and the fear he inspires. When I come into his presence to secure his support for measures of this kind I cannot, as canon law requires, avoid personal contact with such men. All I can do is to avoid condoning their conduct. I am afraid of contracting sin by associating with them, for I remember that at the time of my consecration I took an oath over the body of St. Peter at Pope Gregory's command, promising that if I was unsuccessful in bringing them back to the right path I would avoid their company. On the other hand, if, in avoiding them, I fail to approach the Frankish prince, I fear that my missionary work amongst the people will greatly suffer.

ST. BONIFACE [174]

Boniface reports the establishment of Frankish synods to Archbishop Cuthbert of Canterbury who in that same year 747 had presided over the famous English Synod of Cloveshoe.

To his brother and fellow-bishop, Cuthbert, raised to the dignity of the archiepiscopate, and united to him by the bond of spiritual kinship, Boniface, Legate for Germany and the Catholic and Apostolic Church of Rome, sends greetings of intimate love in Christ.

It is written in the book of Solomon: *Happy is the man who has found a friend with whom he can speak as with himself.* [Ecclus. 25, 12] We have received by the hand of your son, the deacon Cynebert, together with your generous gifts, a delightful and affectionate letter. You have also sent me by him verbally a welcome discourse concerning our fraternal relations. I hope that as long as life shall last this exchange of spiritual counsel may go on, if God wills, from whom alone all holy desires, all good counsel, and all just works do proceed. May you and I be bound together in the golden bonds of heavenly love which cannot be broken, you better and more fully because God has endowed you with greater gifts of knowledge and power, I striving to be instructed as your devoted vassal, *faithful in many things.*

The work of our ministry is in one and the same cause: an equal supervision over Churches and people is entrusted to us, whether in teaching or in reproving or in admonition or in protecting all classes of clergy and laity. Wherefore I humbly request that if at any time God shall inspire you or your synods with wholesome counsel you will not hesitate to share it with me. And I likewise, if God will impart to me in my weakness anything useful or profitable to you, will do the same by you. Our responsibility towards Churches and peoples is greater than that of other bishops on account of the pallium entrusted to us and accepted by us, while they have the care of their own dioceses only. And hence, dear friend (not that you, who are so wise, need to hear or read the decisions of us simple folk), we feel that on account of your holy and humble good will towards us you would like to be informed about the decisions we have taken here and so submit them to you for correction and improvement.

We decided in our synod that we will maintain the Catholic faith and unity and our subjection to the Roman Church as long as we live: that we will be loyal subjects of St. Peter and his vicar; that we will hold a synod every year; that our metropolitan bishops shall ask for their palliums from that see; and that in all things we shall obey the orders of St. Peter according to the canons, so that we may be numbered among the flock entrusted to his care. To these declarations we have all agreed and subscribed, and we have forwarded them to the shrine of St. Peter, prince of the Apostles. The Roman clergy and Pontiff have gratefully accepted them. We have decided that every year the canonical decrees, the laws of the Church, the rule of regular life, shall be read and renewed at the synod. We have decreed that the metropolitan, having received his pallium, shall exhort the other bishops and admonish them and make enquiry as to who among them is watchful over the people's welfare and who is negligent. We have forbidden the clergy to hunt, to go about in the woods with dogs and to keep falcons or hawks.

We have ordered every priest annually during Lent to render to his bishop an account of his ministry, the state of the Catholic faith, Baptism and every detail of his administration. We have decreed that every bishop shall make an annual visitation of his diocese confirming and instructing the people, seeking out and forbidding pagan rites, divination, fortune-telling, soothsaying, charms, incantations and all Gentile vileness. We have forbidden the servants of God to wear showy or martial dress or to carry arms.

We have decreed that it shall be the special duty of the metropolitan to enquire into the conduct of the bishops under him and their care for the people. He shall require them, on their return from the synod, each to hold a meeting in his own diocese with his priests and abbots and urge them to carry out the synodal decrees. And every bishop finding himself unable to reform or correct some fault in his own diocese shall lay the case openly in the synod before the archbishop for correction, just as the Roman Church at my ordination bound me by oath that if I found priests or people wandering from the law of God and could not correct them I would always faithfully report the case to the Apostolic See and the vicar of St. Peter for settlement. Thus, if I am not mistaken, should every bishop do to his metropolitan and to the Roman Pontiff if the case cannot be settled among themselves. So shall they be guiltless of the blood of lost souls.

ST. BONIFACE [175]

Boniface reports to a new Pope, Stephen III (752).

To the most noble lord Pope Stephen, exalted and beloved above all pontiffs, endowed with the privilege of the apostolate, Boniface, a humble bishop and disciple of the Roman Church, sends affectionate greeting of love in Christ.

I pray for Your Holiness from the depths of my heart that I may be worthy to claim and possess that intimate union with the Apostolic See under your gentle sway and to remain your faithful and devoted servant and disciple in the same way I have already served the Apostolic See under three of your predecessors, the two Gregories and Zacharias, of venerable memory, who always helped me and strengthened me with their letters of exhortation and with their authority. I pray Your Grace so to act that I may still more efficiently carry out and fulfil your fatherly intentions. For if I have accomplished anything of value in this Roman mission, in which I have been engaged now these six-and-thirty years, I desire to increase and fulfill it. Or if it be found that I have said or done anything wrong or unwise I pledge myself to correct it humbly and willingly and at once according to the judgment of the Roman Church.

ST. BONIFACE [176]

Abbreviations

Reference Table

Orthodox Church of Christ, New York, 1961, pp. 746, 827, 828.   89

79. Blaise PASCAL, *Pensées,* Number 552, New York, Random House, 1941, pp. 175–178.   91

80. Dietrich BONHOEFFER, *Prisoner for God,* New York, Macmillan, 1961, p. 22.   92

81. HIPPOLYTUS OF ROME, "The Cosmic Tree," in J. Daniélou, *The Advent of Salvation,* New York, The Paulist Press, 1962, p. 136.   93

82. Jean DANIELOU, *The Advent of Salvation,* New York, The Paulist Press, 1962, p. 117.   93

83. Louis BOUYER, *The Paschal Mystery,* London, George Allen & Unwin, 1951, p. xiv.   94

84. Louis BOUYER, *ibid.,* p. 50.   94

85. Gerard S. SLOYAN, *To Hear the Word of God, Homilies at Mass,* New York, Herder and Herder, 1965, pp. 95–98.   97

86. Louis BOUYER, *The Paschal Mystery,* pp. 39–40, 40–42.   98

87. Louis BOUYER, *ibid.,* 175.   99

88. Louis BOUYER, *ibid.,* pp. 177–179.   100

89. Brother ANTONINUS, "Gethsemani," in *The Crooked Lines of God,* Detroit, University of Detroit Press, 1960, pp. 40–41.   101

90. Louis BOUYER, *The Paschal Mystery,* pp. 249.   102

91. Louis BOUYER, *ibid.,* pp. 263–264.   103

92. Edward HOWARD, "We Are Easter Men and Alleluia Is Our Song," *Worship* XXXVIII, IV, March, 1964, pp. 188–189.   104

93. ASTERIUS OF AMASIA, "Homily 19 on Psalm 5," in *Early Christian Prayers,* edited by A. Hamman, Chicago, Henry Regnery Co., 1961, p. 172.   105

94. PASCHAL VIGIL, Easter Exultation in the *Roman Missal.*   105

95. ST. JOHN CHRYSOSTOM, "Homily on Drunkenness," in *PG* 50, 438.   110

96. HIPPOLYTUS OF ROME, "Homily 6 for Easter," in

220

SANCTORAL

223